VISUAL RESOURCES
An International Journal of Documentation

Vol. XI, No. 1

1995

EDITOR: Helene E. Roberts
Dartmouth College

TECHNOLOGY EDITOR: Christine L. Sundt
University of Oregon

REVIEW EDITOR: Elizabeth O'Donnell
Dartmouth College

BIBLIOGRAPHER: Patricia L. Keats
California Historical Society

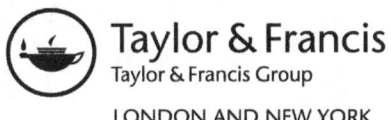

Taylor & Francis Group

LONDON AND NEW YORK

VISUAL RESOURCES
An International Journal of Documentation
Vol. XI, No. 1, 1995

TABLE OF CONTENTS

SPECIAL ISSUE OF *VISUAL RESOURCES*

IMAGES IN LIBRARIES, MUSEUMS, AND ARCHIVES: DESCRIPTION AND INTELLECTUAL ACCESS: PAPERS FROM THE PHILADELPHIA AREA CONSORTIUM OF SPECIAL COLLECTIONS LIBRARIES (PACSCL) SUMMER SEMINAR, 1993, Edited by Amy M. McColl

3   Amy M. McColl, *Introduction*

5   Georgia B. Barnhill, *Pictorial Histories of the United States*

21 Katherine Martinez, *Imaging the Past: Historians, Visual Images and the Contested Definition of History*

47 Marcy Flynn and Helena Zinkham, *The MARC Format and Electronic Reference Images: Experiences from the Library of Congress Prints and Photographs Division*

71 Michael Joseph, *Information Technology and Access to Visual Images in Printed Books*

85 Jackie M. Dooley, *Processing and Cataloguing of Archival Photograph Collections*

103 William H. Helfand, *The Search for Ephemera Images*

CONTRIBUTORS

Georgia Brady Barnhill has been the Andrew W. Mellon Curator of Graphic Arts at the American Antiquarian Society for twenty-five years. She is particularly interested in the history of American book illustration and nineteenth-century prints. Currently she is serving as guest curator at the Adirondack Museum in New York State for an exhibition of their print collection, *Wild Impressions: The Adirondacks on Paper*. Another continuing project is the compilation of a bibliography on eighteenth- and nineteenth-century American prints and illustrations under the auspices of the American Historical Print Collectors Society.

Jackie Dooley is Head of Special Collections and University Archives at the University of California, Irvine. Previously she has held positions with visual collections at the Getty Center for the History of Art and the Humanities, the Library of Congress, and the University of California, San Diego. She is active in organizations supporting the preservation and documentation of visual collections and has published papers on topics such as authority control, subject analysis for archival materials, and rare book cataloguing.

Marcy Silver Flynn has served in the Prints and Photographs Division of the Maryland Historical Society and the Historical Society of Pennsylvania. From 1991 through 1994, she was a cataloguer in the Processing Section of the Prints and Photographs Division of the Library of Congress. She recently founded Silver Image Management, a consulting firm which specializes in providing collections management services for institutions and individuals with holdings of visual materials.

William H. Helfand is a consultant to the National Library of Medicine, the Philadelphia Museum of Art, and other institutions in areas relating to art and medicine. He has published a number of books and articles on the history of pharmacy and on his collecting interests which include prints, caricatures, posters, postcards, and other ephemera which relate to medicine and pharmacy.

Michael Scott Joseph, the Rare Book and Jerseyana Catalog Librarian at Rutgers, the State University of New Jersey, is best known for his work on wood engraving and children's book illustrations in the mid-nineteenth century American book trade. Currently he is at work on a history of the early American picture-book from 1800–1880, and on a bibliography of books illustrated with woodblocks by the McLoughlin Brothers of New York.

Katherine Martinez, the Curator of American and British History at the Stanford University Libraries, was formerly the Director of Advanced Studies at the Winterthur Museum and Director of the Winterthur Library. She has also held library positions at the Cooper-Hewitt Museum, Columbia University, and the Smithsonian Institution.

Amy McColl began as a cataloguer at the Biddle Law Library of the University of Pennsylvania. In 1991, she took the position of Name Authority Coordinator for the Philadelphia Area Consortium of Special Collections Libraries (PACSCL), and in 1993 became Project Coordinator of PACSCL's grant-funded cataloguing and authorities project. She has also served on various ALA and LC committees and task groups, including the Cooperative Cataloguing Council's Task Group on Authorities. She is the author of the Library of Congress NACC Participants' Manual.

Helena Zinkham has worked with collections of visual materials at both the Maryland Historical Society and the New York Historical Society. She is currently head of processing and cataloging at the Library of Congress Prints and Photographs Division, where many projects involving electronic surrogates and automated catalogs have been completed during the past decade.

A SPECIAL ISSUE OF
VISUAL RESOURCES

Images in Libraries, Museums, and Archives:
Description and Intellectual Access

*Papers from PACSCL
(The Philadelphia Area Consortium
of Special Collections Libraries)*

Summer Seminar, 1993

*Edited by
AMY M. McCOLL*

Introduction

by Amy M. McColl

In August of 1993, the Philadelphia Area Consortium of Special Collections Libraries (PACSCL) sponsored the second of its annual summer seminars. The topic was "Images in Libraries, Museums, and Archives: Description and Intellectual Access," and the seminar was attended by approximately 80 participants from around the United States and Canada. Speakers addressed issues and current practice of describing and accessing illustrative matter, and geared their talks towards experienced graphic arts curators, special collections librarians, and archivists.

Several of the papers given during the PACSCL seminar are included in this special issue of *Visual Resources* in the hopes of reaching a larger audience. Georgia Barnhill of the American Antiquarian Society addresses the history of 19th- and early 20th-century pictorial histories, and discusses ways in which researchers might use them more effectively. Katharine Martinez of Stanford University gives a researcher's point of view on the intellectual access to images in libraries and archival collections. Marcy Silver Flynn and Helena Zinkham of the Library of Congress discuss ongoing projects at LC designed to give better access to the images in its vast collection. Michael Joseph of Rutgers University speaks of the particular problems faced by librarians and researchers with regard to description and access to book illustrations. Jackie Dooley, formerly of the Getty Center for the History of Art and the Humanities and currently Head of Special Collections at the University of California, Irvine, details access to photographic collections. Finally, William Helfand describes the thorny problems encountered by researchers in accessing ephemera.

The papers generated much discussion during the seminar. Topics included the use of images as evidence, as well as the uses of digital imaging technology to improve access to images. Vendors were on hand to demonstrate several systems. While all agreed that this technology is definitely desirable and the wave of the future, cost and budgetary issues were cited as hindrances to the speedy adoption of digital imaging systems by many librarians and curators. The seminar offered many opportunities for continued discussions among speakers and participants at two evening receptions and a closing luncheon.

PACSCL is an incorporated not-for-profit organization of twenty institutions—both public and private—in the Delaware Valley. The Consortium is dedicated to the notion that the whole is greater than the sum of its parts and that through collaboration, cooperation, and coordination, member institutions can enhance services, facilitate learning, and increase support in ways they could not alone. PACSCL was founded in 1985, and the summer seminars series was begun in 1992. By sponsoring an annual seminar focusing on the "hot issues" of the day for librarians, archivists, and other information specialists and their clients, we hope to extend the opportunity for continuing education and communication between experts and professionals in the special collections community.

PACSCL would like to extend its gratitude to the editors of *Visual Resources*, most especially Helene Roberts, for agreeing to publish these papers from the 1993 seminar in this special issue. We are pleased that the proceedings will reach a greater number of graphic arts enthusiasts and professionals through this medium.

Pictorial Histories of the United States

by Georgia B. Barnhill

> We belong to a generation that has no time to read its Gibbon but will linger fascinated over a thousand images of history ... The selection and interpretation of these pictures is a new art and constitutes a visual-literary form as revolutionary in our time as was the novel in the eighteenth century and the short story in the nineteenth. Today we are on the threshold of an even greater revolution whereby the eyes and ears of the world are being brought within the family through cinema and television. We are expanding the borders of Gutenberg's world beyond the setting of movable type.
>
> (Francis Henry Taylor, 1951)

Taylor wrote these words in his foreword to Marshall Davidson's *Life in America*, one of the best modern popular pictorial histories of the United States.[1] Sinclair Hitchings, keeper of prints at the Boston Public Library, used this quotation on a leaflet he produced over twenty years ago addressed to writers, publishers, and librarians. In it, Hitchings bemoaned the visual illiteracy of historians, publishers, picture researchers, and even librarians, none of whom seemed able to respond to the "new art" of presenting and interpreting pictures. He recommended that the professional picture researcher have a background in art history and "an acquaintance with four important classes of material—pictorial histories; illustrated exhibition catalogues; catalogues of collections; and bibliographies." More recently Hitchings has written,

> The art and craft of pictorial history is seldom understood, rarely mastered, and yet to be taught. It requires a skillful weaving-together of pictures and words to present facts and insights which open to us some part of the past. A clearly defined theme, mastery of detail, and command of many sources must be combined with book design informed by special experience, if this approach to history is to succeed.[2]

Curators and librarians are destined to assist scholars and picture researchers in their effort to provide images for texts, films, and the various electronic media that are now being devised. How can we do this effectively? Sinclair Hitchings suggested that researchers needed to be familiar with four classes of material. This essay will focus on the first of those—pictorial histories.

The lack of access to images in books and periodicals is a situation that we should remedy because our collections contain so much visual material that has not been fully exploited. Since our institutions continue to spend large sums of money to acquire, house, care for, and service these collections, it is extremely important that these collections are appropriately described and that there is adequate intellectual access to them. Moreover, as Francis Henry Taylor observed over forty years ago, the public clamors for pictures, but not for words. This characteristic of twentieth-century society increases the pressures upon us.

The images that we as curators and archivists provide to those who want them, for whatever reason, are a factor in the quality of the final product. The better access we provide to collections, the wider and better is the choice for those who come to us. Much of my work each day involves responding to inquiries from picture researchers who work for book publishers and film producers. I admit to a great deal of frustration in this part of my job. Many want eye-witness depictions of events in color, but they cannot leave their desks whether located in Boston, New York, or Orlando because of budgetary or time constraints. They seem not to care whether the depiction has any truth to it or if it is a total fabrication. And their deadline was the day before yesterday. I am sure that many curators have had the same experiences and that none of this is new to those of you who work in public services. There is an obvious need for assistance on a large scale.

Discussing traditional means of access in the world of electronic databases and videodisc presentations of collections seems archaic, but the future is not the present yet. We still need to guide users of our collections and this essay offers three suggestions The Catalogue of American Engravings at the American Antiquarian Society provides access to over 16,000 engravings issued in the United States prior to the year 1821. A second suggestion follows the recommendation made by Hitchings a generation ago that picture researchers become acquainted with pictorial histories. There are several nineteenth-century authors and illustrators whose works are based on first-hand knowledge and thus are valid documents. Finally, in the present century, several publications can serve as both sources and models for picture researchers.

At the American Antiquarian Society, one component of our new on-line catalogue is the Catalogue of American Engravings, a revision and supplement to the Stauffer and Fielding lists of American Engravings published early in the twentieth century. Funded over a fifteen year period by the National Endowment for the Humanities, the H.W. Wilson Foundation, and most recently by the Getty Grant Program, this Catalogue describes over 16,000 book illustrations and separately published prints issued prior to 1821. Access by artist, engraver, publisher, subject, genre, place and date of publication is possible. The thesaurus of subject headings includes over 7,000 terms. Over ninety percent of the engravings are book and periodical illustrations. For them we cite the author and title of the publication providing for the first time the full context for each illustration. This is a union catalogue containing information on the holdings of other libraries and museums. Each entry includes the technique, format, dimensions, exact transcription of the title, differences between states, and a description of the visual content of the image. The location of one impression of each engraving is noted. Unfortunately, the Catalogue of American Engravings Project began in earnest many years ago and images were not incorporated with the cataloguing records. We may, however, try to remedy this in the future. Picture researchers and historians can find many images of historical significance using this database and we use it frequently for this purpose. The Catalogue is available on the Internet via the AAS Gopher. Providing such detailed records for book illustrations is expensive. However, for the first time, researchers can quickly locate appropriate visual materials for whatever reason. This project can serve as a model for future cataloguing endeavors.

A number of illustrated popular histories were published during the nineteenth century. The works of three authors, John Warner Barber, Benson John Lossing, and Jesse Ames Spencer, are common, and the illustrators were all seeking to produce illustrations faithful to historical fact. No one has indexed the illustrations in these volumes, but researchers looking for images should be directed to them.

One of the first authors of illustrated pictorial histories of the United States was John Warner Barber. Born in Windsor, Connecticut, in 1798, he was the son of a farmer of modest circumstances. Although later in life he denied having much formal education, he was enrolled for at least some time at the Windsor Academy in 1808. Among his childhood reading was the Bible, Bunyan's *Pilgrim Progress, The New England Primer,* and Mrs. Barbauld's popular compilation, *Hymns.* He owned a copy of a chapbook, *Lazy Lawrence,* that he purchased in Hartford in 1806. At the age of ten, he was already copying illustrations from chapbooks so we know that images appealed to him at an early age. Two sets of sketchbooks at the Beinecke Library at Yale University suggest that at a very early age he was trying to create children's books on historical subjects.[3]

At the age of fifteen, shortly after the death of his father, Barber was apprenticed to the engraver Abner Reed, active in East Windsor. Barber started to keep a diary at that time and continued the practice until his death. Among the titles that he read were *Stranger in Ireland*, *Christian Memoir*, and *Mather's Life*. This last title suggests his interest in history. Among the engravings that he did while an apprentice were the plates for *The Naval Temple* designed by Michel Felice Corné (ca. 1752–1845) and Elkanah Tisdale (1768–1835), a Connecticut illustrator and engraver then living in Boston. After his apprenticeship, Barber settled in New Haven where he lived and worked for over sixty years.

One of the first historical works that Barber wrote and illustrated was his *Views of New Haven and Its Vicinity* published by Barber and A. H. Maltby in 1825. This book is charmingly illustrated with views of New Haven, but they are views and not depictions of events.

Three years later, Barber published his first pictorial history of the United States. Barber compiled *Interesting Events in the History of the United States* from the "most approved Authorities." It is illustrated with sixteen engraved plates, three images to a page. Each image is numbered and keyed to a paragraph in the text. The preface provides Barber's reasons for compiling this text:

> In a country like ours, it seems necessary to the existence of true and enlightened patriotism, that every person should possess some knowledge of the history of his own country. By the aid of history, we can call up past scenes and events in review—we can see the effects they have had upon the nations before us, and from thence we can learn wisdom for the future.[4]

He continues by noting that this book is not for those already knowledgeable about the history of the United States, but is for those "who cannot spare the time or expense of reading or procuring a full and complete history."[5] He thought the volume would be useful as a reference book, for there is a chronology at the end to record relatively minor events. He concluded by stating that the "numerous engravings interspersed through the book, it is thought will be of utility in making the work interesting, and of fixing the facts more firmly in the mind."[6] This role for images within an historical text is very important. Not only should the images make the text more interesting, but they help the reader remember the facts. The images in this book, small copperplate engravings, are naive in style and quaint. They do relate perfectly to the text, however, and play a role within it as stated in the preface. Barber's work was designed to be both a popular and pictorial history, a genre that continues to this day. The text remained in print for some years. The copy of the 1831 edition at the American Antiquarian Society belonged to the great twentieth-century historian, Samuel Eliot Morison. The text of the 1831 edition is expanded, but the illustrations remain the same.

Barber's *History and Antiquities of New Haven* published by him in 1831 reused the illustrations that he published in his first book about New Haven. He added an engraving of the *Battle of Lexington* that he copied from Amos Doolittle's engraving of the scene based on the design of Ralph Earl, one of the participants. In fact, Doolittle was present as well. Barber recognized the significance of the eye-witness account by describing the print as the "first regular historical print ever published in America."[7] With the engraving, Barber reprints a lengthy account of the military action, but fails to indicate why the engraving was included in this work on New Haven's history.

Barber went on to write and illustrate important works on the history of Connecticut, Massachusetts, New Jersey, New York, and several other states. He traveled extensively to collect the materials for those works. These books are all illustrated with views of the towns and cities, not with depictions of events. In 1856 and 1857, he and Henry Howe, his sometime collaborator on the earlier volumes, produced *Our Whole Country: or the Past and Present of the United States*. Published in New York in 1861 in two volumes, it contains 605 illustrations, a substantial number when compared to publications earlier in the century. Barber notes that "care was taken that every engraving should be truthful; and as the work intends to be one of *facts only*, fancy sketches and artistic representations merely have been avoided in the text."[8] Some of the views are derived from earlier ones, but many of them have been updated. Some illustrations focus on commerce and transportation while others introduce topics such as tourism. The illustrations in this work are different in scope from his 1828 publication. The text discusses events, but the images focus on places and commerce.

American Scenes published in 1868 returns to the earlier formula. (Figure 1) Barber notes that the object of the work "is to present to the reader a series of Historical Incidents in American History, (some of which may not be generally known,) in an *historical, pictorial, and poetic* form." It is to be "interesting and instructive."[9] Barber knew the value of images in express-

10 / VISUAL RESOURCES

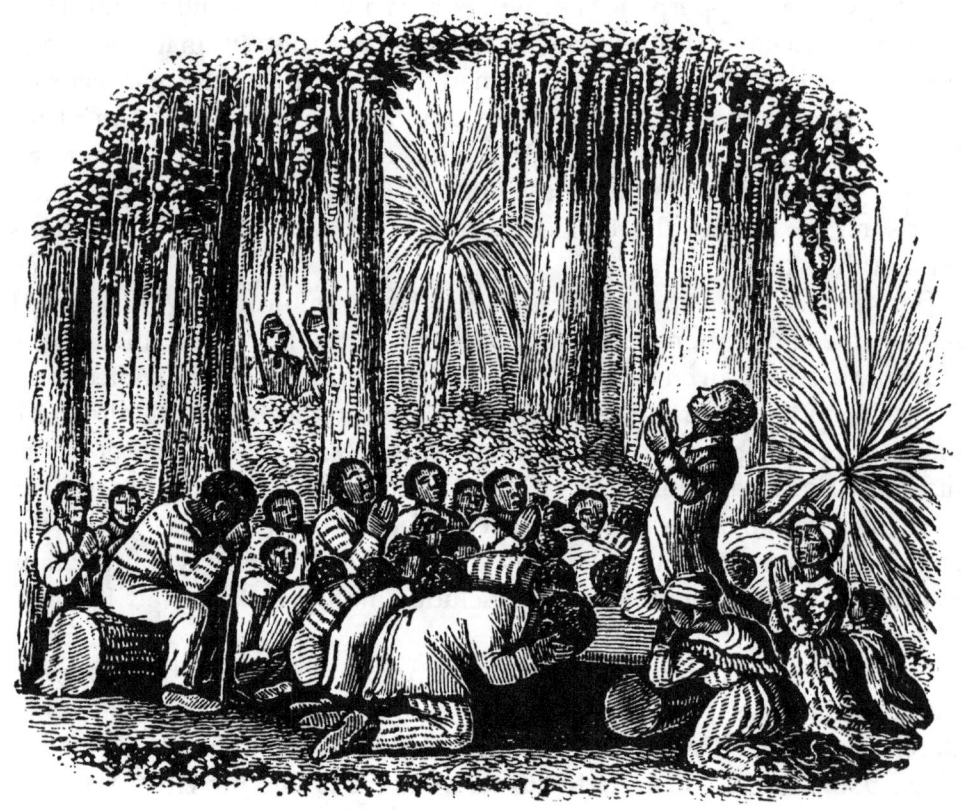

PRAYER-MEETING AMONG THE SLAVES.

Figure 1. "Prayer-Meeting among the Slaves," From John Warner Barber, American Scenes (Springfield, Mass., 1868), p. 205. 2⅜" a 2¾". (Courtesy of the American Antiquarian Society)

ing truths. He was also the author of several religious works including *The Picture Preacher* published in New Haven by Henry Howe in 1880. The publisher wrote in a preface that Barber's object was

> not to make pretty pictures but to enforce some moral truth. Everything is made with studied simplicity to bend to this purpose. Hence they have a peculiar power. They attract by their originality and often create a smile by their quaintness. But they are so bold, so strong, as to tell their story at a single glance; and thus they impress a lesson when elegance and delicacy alone would fail.[10]

Barber had the same goals in mind when he created the illustrations for his histories and I would hazard a guess that publishers today are seeking to "impress a lesson" with their illustrations. Events in Barber's final historical work include *The Attack on Brookfield* depicting a raid on a Massachusetts village during King Philip's War in 1695 and *Prayer Meeting Among the Slaves*.

A second historical writer who integrated illustrations with his own texts was Benson John Lossing (1813–1891). Born in 1813, Lossing was apprenticed to a watchmaker at the age of thirteen after just three years of formal education in the district schools in Beekman, New York. As a young man, he read widely, especially in history. At the age of twenty-two, he became a joint editor and proprietor of the *Poughkeepsie Telegraph*, and later of the *Poughkeepsie Casket*. It was then that he learned to engrave on wood, a skill that he took to New York in 1838 when he established himself there as an engraver on wood. A decade later he decided to write a narrative sketchbook relating to the American Revolution and he traveled more than eight thousand miles gathering material. It was published in parts by Harper & Brothers from 1850 to 1852 and was well received.[11] Although he wrote other histories, those of greatest interest are his three "pictorial field books" of the Revolution, the War of 1812, and the Civil War.

At the time Lossing was writing, he felt confident that most people had a general knowledge of the history of the Revolution. What he felt was lacking was an acquaintance with the locations of the various events and battles. Lossing's goal was to fill this void by traveling thousands of miles to visit important sites and to gather as much information about them as he could by interviewing people who still had first-hand knowledge about that period of American history. In his own words:

> For years a strong desire was felt to embalm those precious things of our cherished household, that they might be preserved for the admiration and reverence of remote posterity. I knew that the genius of our people was the reverse of antiquarian reverence for the things of the past; that the glowing future, all sunlight and eminence, absorbed their thoughts and energies, and few looked back to the twilight and dim valleys of the part through which they had journeyed.[12]

His goal was a noble one. Of his pictures he wrote: "Special care has been observed to make faithful delineations of fact. If a relic of the Revolution was not susceptible of picturesque effect in a drawing, without a departure from truth, it has been left in its plainness, for my chief object was to illustrate the subject, not merely to embellish the book."[13] Among the illustrations are depictions of battle scenes supplemented with battle plans generally copied from British sources. Lossing did not constantly focus on the experiences of the great men, as many other historians have done between his day and ours, but included the portrait of Isaac Rice, for example, a participant at the Battle of Saratoga and Lossing's guide at Fort Ticonderoga, the ruins of which are also depicted. (Figure 2)

12 / VISUAL RESOURCES

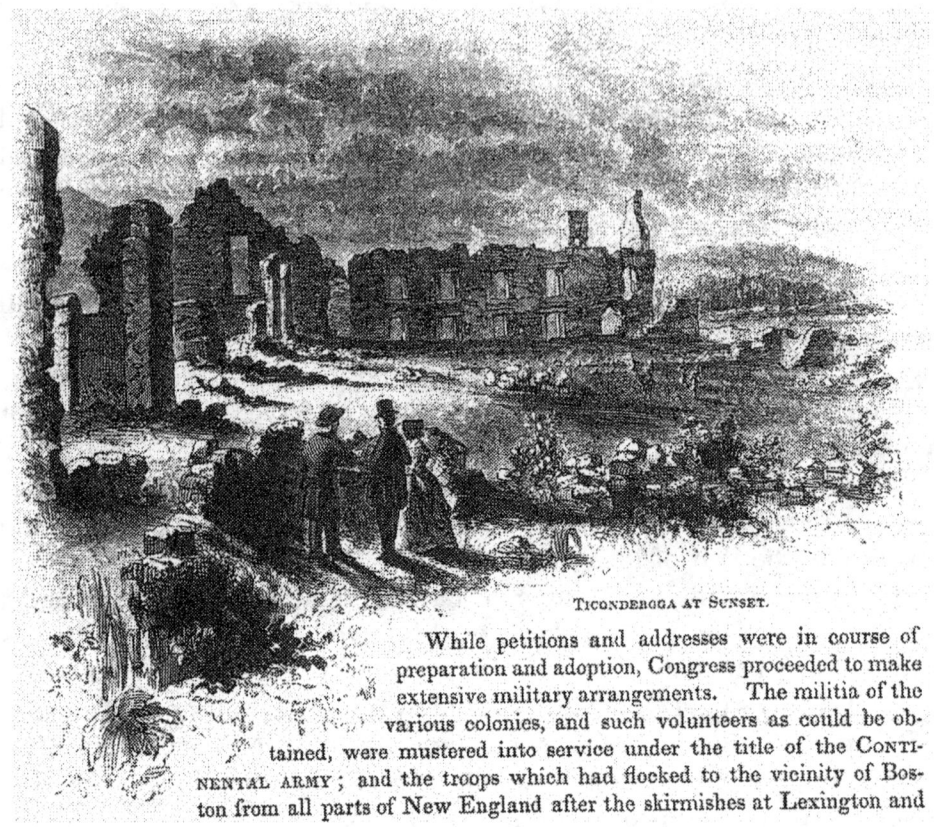

Figure 2. "Ticonderoga at Sunset," From Benson J. Lossing, The Pictorial Field-Book of the United States (New York, 1851), Vol. 1, p. 127. 4⅛" × 4¾". (Courtesy of the American Antiquarian Society)

For his *Field Book of the War of 1812* published in 1868 again by Harper & Brothers in New York, Lossing traveled more than ten thousand miles in the United States and Canada "gathering up, recording, and delineating every thing of special value, not found in books, illustrative of the subject, and making himself familiar with the topography and incidents of the battlefields of that war." He visited archives and libraries and "from the lips of actors in the events of that struggle he received the most interesting information concerning it, which might have perished with them."[14]

The choice of illustrative material is idiosyncratic, as we shall see. An illustration relating to the confrontation between General Arthur St. Clair and the tribe of the Miami Indians near Fort Wayne, Indiana, in 1790, is of an apple tree near the Indian camp, sketched during his visit to the region in 1860. This tree was planted by a French trader in the first half of the eighteenth century. However, the Plan of St. Clair's Camp and Battle was copied from a contemporary journal of the campaign kept by Winthrop Sargent of Philadelphia. It shows the disposition of the various troops and their enemies. Illustrations such as these show a combination of nostalgia for the past and the presentation of historically accurate information.

Lossing's *Pictorial History of the Civil War in the United States of America* was published in thirty parts from 1866 to 1868, with some thirteen hundred illustrations on wood and steel. He worked on this *History* during the War itself and he had the full cooperation of Union authorities and Lincoln's own blessing on the project which gave him access to official documents. He visited major and minor battlefields and interviewed civilian and military leaders on both sides of the conflict. He wrote in the preface that "the engravings, whilst they embellish the book, have been introduced for the higher purposes of instruction, and are confined to the service of illustrating facts. They have been prepared under my direct supervision; and great pains have been taken to make them correct delineations of the objects sought to be represented." He noted his indebtedness to the publishers of *Harper's Weekly* and *Frank Leslie's Illustrated Newspaper* for he based some of his own illustrations on the eyewitness illustrations that appeared in the pages of those two journals during the War.[15] Among the illustrations is the *Battle of Antietam—Taking of the Bridge on Antietam Creek*, which is a heroic depiction of an important moment in that long battle. The *Evacuation of Cumberland Gap* looks more like a distant view of fireworks than the aftermath of a battle, but troops are marching by the light of the moon through a broad valley. *General Lyons Charge at the Battle of Wilsons Creek* was designed by the artist Felix Octavius Carr Darley. Again, the heroics of the Union leaders and soldiers are highlighted. The two wood engravings of Cairo, Illinois, at the confluence of the Ohio and Mississippi Rivers, show the situation of the town between the two mighty rivers. Lossing attempted in his pictorial histories to weave past and present together in an interesting way. Lossing's insistence on accuracy is convincing and his depictions are probably trustworthy. As in Barber's case, Lossing was both author and illustrator and exercised considerable control over the final product.

A third nineteenth-century historian was Jesse Ames Spencer, who was born in Hyde Park, New York, in 1816. At the age of fourteen he moved with his family to New York City where he went to work in a printing office. Having mastered the art of printing, he assisted his father who was a surveyor and then attended Columbia College, graduating in 1837. Subsequently he attended the Episcopal General Theological Seminary where he was graduated in 1840. A spell of ill health forced him to travel extensively. In the 1850s he was employed as secretary and editor of the General

Protestant Episcopal Sunday-School Union and Church Book Society. Later he became rector of a church in Brooklyn and then a professor of Greek in the College of the City of New York. He wrote a number of theological works, educational texts, travel accounts, and a *History of the United States* published by the firm of Johnson, Fry, and Company in New York in 1867.[16] This work is illustrated with steel engravings after designs by Alonzo Chappel, Emanuel Leutze, Thomas Nast, and other artists. From the preface, it seems that Spencer left the matter of illustration entirely up to the publishers, who according to him, "have zealously labored to secure the best service possible, and to present to the American public a work which, they believe, is unequalled in the spirit and beauty of its illustrations, and the elegance of its typography."[17] The illustrations from this book certainly abound in my own institution's collection of miscellaneous portrait prints and in the collection of historical scenes. Long since removed from their publications, I have always been suspicious of Chappel's work, assuming that his designs were always fictitious. It seems, however, that he too based his illustrations on a considerable amount of research, particularly in written sources.[18] He also used extant portraits for the figures in engravings such as *Drafting the Declaration of Independence*. Since Chappel prepared most of the designs, his contributions to this work will be described.

Chappel often chose to focus on the action of a battle rather than select the distant point of view of earlier artists who drew, for example, two ships battling, rather than the arm-to-arm combat that often occurred even in naval battles. Examples include the *Battle of Lake Champlain—McDonough's Victory* and *The Battle of New Orleans*.

Although some battle scenes are completely sanitized, occasionally Chappel does include a less idealized view of a battle. The *Battle of Gettysburg* shows the carnage as seen at the rear of the battle—men and horses killed, men pulling the artillery piece instead of a draft animal. (Figure 3) The engraving, however, lacks the realism of photographs by Mathew Brady and other photographers at the fronts. Of course, the age of photographing action was still in the future, so photographs taken during the Civil War show the aftermath of battle, not the battle itself.

Alonzo Chappel was born in New York in 1828. Even as a youngster, the self-taught artist painted portraits for modest sums. He studied for just a year at the National Academy of Design. Unlike other illustrators, Chappel began and maintained a working relationship with one publishing firm and its various successors which began as Martin, Johnson, and Company. It published many historical works illustrated by Chappel. There is no evidence that Chappel or other artists whose works were included in Spencer's

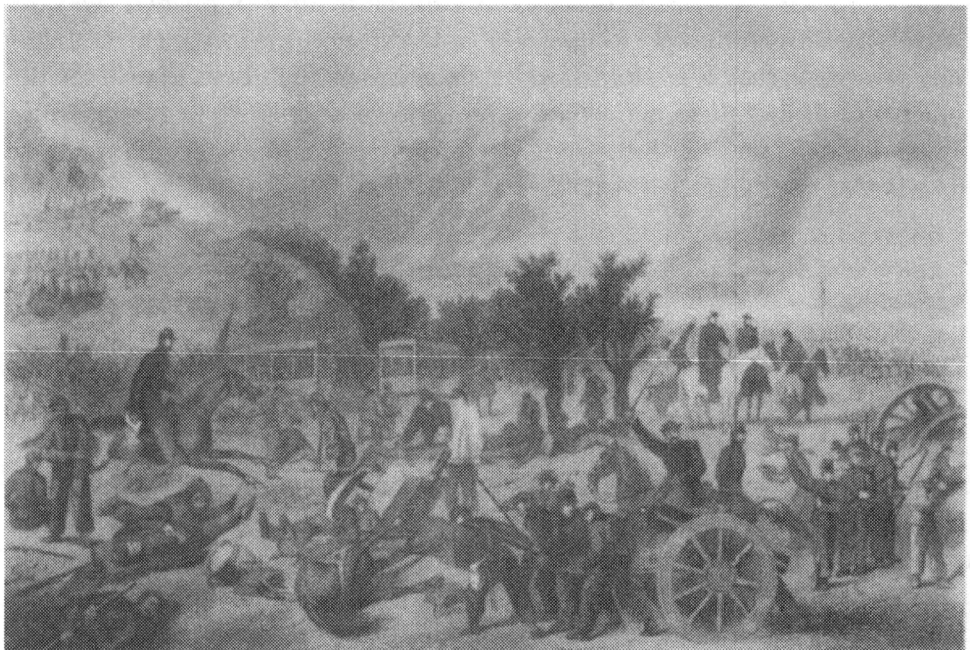

Figure 3. "*Battle of Gettysburg,*" *From Jesse A. Spencer,* History of the United States *(New York, 1866), Vol. 4, facing p. 333. 5¼" × 7½". (Courtesy of the American Antiquarian Society)*

History traveled the way Barber and Lossing did to sites. Nor is there any special collaboration evident between the author and the artists who provided illustrations for this publication. This is the pattern for most later publications of American history.

The works of Barber, Lossing, and Spencer should be used judiciously by scholars and picture researchers. Perhaps these volumes remain unused on the shelves because there are no projects like the Catalogue of American Engravings for the nineteenth century. There is a rich body of pictorial material, but no access to it.

Having looked at the nineteenth-century beginnings of popular pictorial histories, we are now going to look at several twentieth-century publications. Tremendous changes took place in the publishing of books, largely due to photographic and reproductive processes. Rather than commission illustrators, publishers purchased copies of historical documents, prints, and photographs. The audience for American history had grown and publishers differentiated among and targeted specific audiences—students, scholars, and the general public. Many of these books provide a world of images for today's researchers.

The Pageant of America was a fifteen volume history published by Yale University Press from 1925 to 1929. The first nine volumes were chronologically arranged; they were followed by six volumes that focused on specific topics such as literature, art, theater, architecture, and sport. In a letter from Oliver McKee, one of the assistant editors, to Clarence Brigham, then librarian of the American Antiquarian Society, McKee wrote:

> the emphasis has been given to a pictorial treatment with a view of making the essentials of American history easier of comprehension to the general reader as well as to supply a useful adjunct to the work of the teacher of history in the schools. It will contain more than ten thousand illustrations, and I think you know something of the extraordinary care we have taken to locate and reproduce pictures having reasonable claims to authenticity.

The text is a combination of running commentary and lengthy captions for the illustrations that were drawn from a long list of museums, libraries, and archives in this country and abroad. This was a team effort with a number of writers and editors. Unfortunately, each page suggests a cut and paste job, but it was a significant achievement, and one that is ignored today, at least in my library. This is one of those monumental works that should be used.

Three authors wrote and gathered illustrations for their own volumes. The results of this kind of control are excellent and recall the efforts of Barber and Lossing. Stefan Lorant, born in Hungary in 1901, was arrested and sent to a concentration camp in 1935 when he was the editor of the *Munich Illustrated Press*. After his release he went to England and then came to the United States in 1940. Before the publication of *The Presidency* by The Macmillan Company in 1951, he wrote pictorial histories on Franklin Delano Roosevelt and Abraham Lincoln. He spent seven years working on *The Presidency*, which contains portraits, statistics, political cartoons, facsimiles of campaign documents of every type, and pictures of conventions, inaugurations, and other presidential events. This volume is richly illustrated and should be used by picture researchers, particularly those who shy away from political prints because of their complex symbolism, and historians of American politics. Stefan Lorant's collection of photographs is now at the Getty Center for the History of Art and the Humanities.

The American Past is another work by a single author. Roger Butterfield was born in 1907 near Rochester, New York. Both parents were school teachers. After graduation from the University of Rochester at the age of nineteen, he worked in Philadelphia for *The Evening Bulletin* and *The Evening Public Ledger*. Later he moved to New York and eventually joined the staff of *Life* magazine. To complete *The American Past* published in 1947, he left *Life* and worked from then on for a number of publishers as a freelance writer. Later he moved to the family homestead in Hartwick, New York, where he happily settled amongst his large collection of American social history, illustrated books, and nineteenth-century illustrated magazines. He sold this collection to the New York Historical Association in Cooperstown and then a few years later became an antiquarian book dealer. His *The American Past* is illustrated with a thousand images covering the period 1775 to 1945. In his foreword he wrote:

> This book was planned and written as a history of American politics—by which I mean considerably more than party conventions and ward heeling and Boss Tweed. Politics, as I understand it, is the proper word for history in action: it includes everything that importantly influences the fate or mood of the nation at any particular time ... Two great impulses—the desire to see all men free and equal, and the desire to be richer and stronger than anyone else—have run through our politics for 170 years, and explain much that has happened in the American past.[19]

Butterfield's book is creatively and wonderfully illustrated. Like Lorant, he was able to weave his text around the illustrations and the result is a coherent whole. He was able to explain the complexities of political cartoons by putting them in their appropriate historical context. This ability eludes users of political prints today, particularly those working in film, because the images are too complex for most viewers.

This book, however, has one major flaw. Butterfield did not credit material from his own collection which means that the illustrations from the pictorial magazines, and there are many of them, are reproduced without citations to the names of the journals or the date of publication. This is frustrating for those of us who encourage picture researchers to use this as a source of illustrations for their works. Illustrations must be properly described to be useful to other researchers.

Finally, we come to Marshall Davidson. He was born in New York in 1907 and was educated at Princeton University. He worked as the associate curator of the American Wing at the Metropolitan Museum of Art from 1935 to 1947 and then served the Museum as editor until 1961. He then was associated with *American Heritage* and Horizon Books for many years. While a curator, he began a project for Houghton Mifflin in which he wished to

> produce a picture of American life as a whole—a picture composed of many pictures—which would glow with the sombre integrity of an Eakins and ring with the joyousness of Whitman. It was a task that required not only a passionate interest in American history and literature but a conversability with the traditional art and artifacts of our people.[20]

Clarence Brigham, director of the American Antiquarian Society at the time, noted in his 1946 annual report that Davidson had worked intensively in the library. He described him as the "only student of the subject who has taken the time himself to visit the libraries and museums of the country to locate material." Davidson's *Life in America* contains a wide selection of visual material in all media and is particularly good for social history.

In 1983 Harry N. Abrams published Davidson's *The Drawing of America: Eyewitness to History*. It is a magnificent book that focuses on the ability of drawings,

> whatever their aesthetic merit, to speak for themselves in elucidating the story of this country—its people and its places—in a direct and immediate way. Their special importance here is that they are one-of-a-kind, on-the-spot, eyewitness documents. Such pictorial reporting can often evoke aspects of experience that can be recalled in no other way; for the arts can sometimes speak to us when written histories remain dumb.[21]

Again, the unity of the images and the text contributes to the success of the volume. Davidson knew what to select and how to use the material appropriately.

This survey suggests that there are publications of the nineteenth and twentieth centuries of immense value to those looking for images. The illustrations in the histories of the nineteenth century are in fact carefully researched. Curiously, however, with the exception of the one print copied by Barber, nineteenth-century authors of popular histories did not seem to have any knowledge about images produced in the eighteenth and early nineteenth centuries. Lorant, Butterfield, and Davidson produced works of lasting value because the illustrations are at the core. They realized the ability of prints to "fix the facts more firmly in the mind," an observation made by Barber and one that should not be forgotten.

The future, however, brings new demands and new technologies. The future will certainly reside in the digitization of images and their publication as video disks and CD/Roms. Other images will find their way onto screens through the Internet. The American Antiquarian Society has already been approached by one corporation to provide 2,000 images for digitization and eventual use on interactive cable TV. The actual implementation of such a system is but a few years away. What is the subject suggested to us? A general pictorial history of the United States! Perhaps I shall pull out Barber's 1828 *History* to use as a guide. As public television supplants reading for intellectual stimulation, the need for images will increase, and indeed is increasing, dramatically. Where one or two images sufficed, a dozen are now needed. The problems that Barber, Lossing, Chappel, and their twentieth-century counterparts encountered are magnified dramatically. The images are available in our libraries; access to them is the problem.

NOTES

1. Marshall B. Davidson, *Life in America* (Boston: Houghton Mifflin Company, 1951), 2 vols., p. vii.
2. Dale Roylance, *American Graphic Arts. A Chronology to 1900 in Books, Prints, and Drawings* (Princeton: Princeton University Library, 1900), p. ix.
3. Information on Barber can be found in Richard Hegel's sketch about him in *American Historians, 1607–1865*, edited by Clyde N. Wilson, vol. 30 in the *Dictionary of Literary Biography* (Detroit: Gale Research Company, 1984). Donald C. O'Brien's paper on Abner Reed, "The Workshop of Abner Reed," presented at a symposium at the American Antiquarian Society in 1993, provided some additional information on Barber. Chauncey C. Nash, *John Warner and His Books* (Milton, Mass., 1934) and Christopher P. Bickford and J. Bard McNulty's *John Warner Barber's Views of Connecticut Towns 1834–36* (Hartford: The Acorn Club, 1990) also provide information on Barber and his work as an historian.
4. Barber, *Interesting Events*, p. iv.
5. *Ibid.*
6. *Ibid.*, p. v.
7. Barber, *History and Antiquities of New Haven, (Conn.)* (New Haven: J. W. Barber, 1831), p. 111.
8. John Warner Barber and Henry Howe, *Our Whole Country: Or the Past and Present of the United States* (New York: George F. Tuttle and Henry M'Cauley, 1861), vol. 1, p. vi.
9. John W. Barber and Elizabeth G. Barber, *American Scenes: Being a Selection of the Most Interesting Incidents in American History* (Springfield, Mass.: D. E. Fisk & Co., 1868), p. 3.
10. John W. Barber, *The Picture Preacher* (New Haven: Henry Howe, 1880), pp. 3–4.
11. For further information on Lossing, see J. Tracy Power's sketch on him in Wilson's *American Historians*, pp. 163–168.
12. Benson J. Lossing, *The Pictorial Field-Book of the Revolution* (New York: Harper & Brothers, 1851), p. iv.
13. Lossing, *Pictorial Field-Book*, p. vi.
14. Benson J. Lossing, *The Pictorial Field-Book of the War of 1812* (New York: Harper & Brothers, 1868), p. i.
15. Benson J. Lossing, *The Pictorial History of The Civil War in the United States of America* (Philadelphia: George W. Childs, 1866), vol. I, p. 5.
16. Information on Spencer may be found in the *Dictionary of American Biography*, vol. 17, pp. 448–9; and in *Appleton's Cyclopaedia of American Biography* (New York: D. Appleton and Company, 1888), vol. 5, p. 630.
17. J. A. Spencer, *History of the United States* (New York: Johnson, Fry and Company, 1866), vol. 1, p. v.
18. Barbara J. Mitnick and David Meschutt, *The Portraits and History Paintings of Alonzo Chappel* (Chadds Ford, Pa.: The Brandywine Museum, 1992), p. 46.
19. Roger Butterfield, *The American Past* (New York: Simon and Schuster, 1947), p. v.
20. Marshall B. Davidson, *Life in America* (Boston: Houghton Mifflin Company, 1951), vol. 1, pp. vii–viii.
21. Marshall B. Davidson, *The Drawing of America* (New York: Harry N. Abrams, 1983), p. 7.

Imaging the Past: Historians, Visual Images and the Contested Definition of History

by Katharine Martinez

> Historical understanding is like a vision, or rather like an evocation of images.
> J. H. Huizinga[1]

HISTORY AS ENTERTAINMENT

Go into any large bookstore, find the history section, and you'll get the impression that historians are in love with pictures. Indeed, experiencing history through pictures in books, magazines, television, and movies is a form of entertainment in America, and history in its many formats is unquestionably a very popular consumer product. In a typical middle-class American home, for example, you are likely to find paperback historical romance novels with lurid covers depicting the embracing hero and heroine in pseudo-period costumes, picture books on the battles of World War II, glossy history magazines such as *American Heritage* and *Civil War History* packed with color pictures, and videos of movies or television programs based on historical figures or events, such as Alex Haley's *Roots*, Ken Burns' *Civil War* and Oliver Stone's *JFK*. Such impressions might even suggest that pictures have replaced written evidence as the most attractive and popular format for most people who want to learn about and enjoy history.

What I have just described is the state of current practice in the field of popular history, that is, history written by journalists, filmmakers, novelists, and free-lance historians for the general public. Pictures are essential in the world of popular history. The walk on the moon, the assassination of President Kennedy, the war in Vietnam were all major historical events that we experienced through pictures. Having grown up with illustrated magazines such as *Time*, *Life*, and *National Geographic*, the middle-class public is visually literate—if not visually sophisticated—and expects to 'read' an historical narrative with the pictures carrying a significant portion of the narrative weight. In contrast, scholarly or academic history has only recently—tentatively—admitted pictures into its realm. The genre of popular history and the genre of academic history rarely intersect.[2] Academic historians often view the magnitude of illustrated popular history with discomfort, condescension, and even some disdain; writing history intended for popular audiences does not 'count' in the process of obtaining tenure.

SCHOLARLY HISTORY

In the world of academia, few historians consult images in their research, and when images appear in scholarly history publications in most cases the images play a secondary role to textual research materials in supporting an argument. Furthermore, the placement of images within illustrated scholarly history books, the quality of the reproductions, and the captions in most cases suggest that images may have been an afterthought, added hurriedly at the last minute to improve the attractiveness of the book once it left the publisher's hands. Why are academic historians so uncomfortable using visual images as evidence? The reasons, I believe, originated in the traditional methods, attitudes, and practices associated with historical scholarship. A preference for textual over visual evidence among academic historians is influenced by how historians are trained, how they view their role as historians, the practice of historical research and writing, plus attitudes towards history and towards visual information. In this article I will discuss the role of images in historical scholarship, and I will describe how librarians, archivists, and curators can promote the use of images as historical evidence.[3]

Attitudes towards images can be reduced to two opposing points of view concerning reality: what one scholar has described as the scientific theory vs. the discourse theory. According to the scientific theory, "there is an external, constant, and absolute reality which can be recorded, measured, and analyzed." In contrast, according to the discourse theory, "each time a viewer experiences an image/text the 'reading' of it can be different."[4] Complicating the debate regarding reality and perception, is the way Western culture views texts and images. Texts are associated with "reason, fact, and objective information," while images are associated with "intuition, art, and implicit knowledge."[5] These two views represent the outer limits of a debate about history, historical evidence, and historical scholarship. Most historians hold positions somewhere in-between. As one historian has noted "... many historians still cling to the opinion that the historian's treatment of documents is scientific or objective in nature while at the same time advocating the traditional notion that history is an art in presentation."[6] With the stage now set, we can begin to flesh out these positions as played out in the world of historical scholarship.

Traditionally, there are two principles on which historical scholarship has been based. These have been questioned and even discredited by recent historians, but their effect is still lingering. The first principle of history scholarship is that history is based on the careful analysis of written records. In *The Literature of American History*, a bibliographic guide published in 1902, the list of materials for the study of American history was organized into Archives and Bibliographies, Collected Documents, Periodicals, and Publications of Societies and Clubs.[7] No mention was made of picture collections. More recent guides to the study of history have expanded the universe of resources to include oral histories, diaries, and statistical data, yet most continue to exclude pictures.[8] The new historians are indeed using a greater variety of documentation, but the use of pictures as historical evidence is certainly not as widespread as statistical data or diaries: written evidence still carries more weight.

The second principle of historical scholarship was the belief that if texts were properly analyzed, history was objective reality. Traditional historians viewed their role as being objective presenters of what actually happened. As one historian stated, history that is of any value should be "allowed to speak for itself."[9] This concern for objectivity influences how historians consider images. A typically skeptical attitude towards images is apparent when you examine the section of "Pictorial Records" in the most recent edition of the *Harvard Guide to American History*, which remains as one of the principle bibliographies for American history:

> Imaginative delineations are least trustworthy historically because of the possibility that the artist, however unintentionally, may have *distorted the truth* (my italics). A classic example is John Trumbull's painting, "The Signing of the Declaration of Independence" (1794), which, though faithfully reproducing the likenesses of the individual participants, misrepresents them as having all attached their signatures at one time. In any event, it is better to consult the originals of paintings or drawings than the engravings, which may have been executed with considerable license. Nonetheless, portraits, photographs, and other graphic representations often provide data in regard to dress, artifacts, and everyday living—the retail traffic of life—that escaped the written records and may even have eluded museum collectors.[10]

This is hardly a hearty recommendation for historians to consider images as legitimate or even trustworthy evidence for their research. The only useful information available in an image had to do with the study of material culture and material life—dress, artifacts, and everyday life—traditionally only anecdotally of interest to scholarly historians. The objective, undistorted truth of what was considered important history was simply not available through images.

New historians, in contrast, acknowledge that the act of writing history involves the historian's point of view, feelings, and attitudes. Objectivity simply is not possible.[11] Yet despite the advent of the new history, a concern for objectivity is still lingering and influencing academic historians. For many, the issue of objectivity is closely tied to their self-identity as historians and tied to the future of the profession. As one writer noted, "... erasing the boundary between fact and fantasy suggests that there is no knowable reality, that it is futile to search for the truth, that verisimilitude is as good as the real thing."[12] In the world of academia, two recent publications elicited intense critical debates about objectivity: Hayden V. White's *Metahistory: The Historical Imagination in Nineteenth-Century Europe* (Baltimore: Johns Hopkins University Press, 1973) and Peter Novick's *That Noble Dream: The 'Objectivity Question' and the American Historical Profession* (Cambridge: Cambridge University Press, 1988).[13] Concurrently, historians are increasingly uncomfortable with the impact media has on the public's understanding of history: "... we are daily assaulted by books, movies and television docu-dramas that hopscotch back and forth between the realms of history and fiction, reality and virtual reality, with impunity."[14] For every documentary film or television program that is judged to be an accurate portrayal of the past, such as *Eyes on the Prize*, there is commercial film, such as *Mississippi Burning*, that is considered to take too much freedom with what historians consider as the historical record.[15] Even worse, digital technology makes it possible to alter photographs and films, and movie directors increasingly take liberties with history, as is most glaringly the case in the recent movie *Forrest Gump*, wherein Tom Hanks appears to have a conversation with President John F. Kennedy.[16]

Even when historians overcame their distrust of images, other challenges created impediments because most historians are not accustomed to consulting picture collections, and most do not have a visual vocabulary of images to draw upon when planning their research. The tendency in most picture collections to organize images by artist rather than subject(s) depicted made the process of finding appropriate visual evidence time-consuming. Today, even when historians are exposed to images in the familiar environment of a historical society, most are still untrained in visual analysis, and lack the ability to recall visual images, make comparisons, and choose among images. Furthermore, most historians still view the world of the image repository as being the property of art historians, a rarefied environment of museums and private collections whose "gatekeepers" are collectors and aesthetes, not fellow scholars or scholar-librarians. Traditional academic historians are more accustomed to working in libraries and archives with written documents and publications, consulting librarians, archivists, and fellow historians. The challenges for historians are the result of traditional attitudes and methodologies, inherent unfamiliarity with other methodologies and fields of study, and academic training.

NEW HISTORY[17]

To contextualize the current use of images by academic historians, let us review the changes that have occurred in the field of history during the last 30 years. When I began my research for this article, I expected to find that the interpretation of images as historical evidence in scholarly publications would coincide with the changes that occurred in academia and in the writing of history beginning in the mid 1960s and early 1970s. Many historians at that time began to dramatically revise their view of history and their roles as historians in response to political and social crises and change: the war in Vietnam, the Civil Rights Movement, the Women's Movement, the murder of the Kennedys and Martin Luther King, and Watergate—events or movements which stimulated academics to question traditionally held attitudes and values concerning America's past, just as they were questioning traditionally held attitudes and values concerning the present and their role in society. The "new history" is characterized by enormous freedom and flexibility: freedom to consider any individual or group or human activity or body of evidence as historically significant. This new attitude towards history and the role of the historian differs from previous practice in four major ways.

Traditionally, history was chiefly concerned with significant events, and the rise and fall of Western nations.

> The new history, on the other hand, has come to be concerned with virtually every human activity ... In the last thirty years we have seen a number of remarkable histories of topics which had not previously been thought to possess a history, for example, childhood, death, madness, the climate, smells, dirt and cleanliness, gestures, the body, femininity, reading, speaking, and even silence."[18]

Secondly, traditional history concentrated on the study of heroes and men of accomplishment—The rest of society played a very minor role in history, if at all. The new historians have focused on individuals and groups that have not been associated with authority, power, or the status-quo, preferring the history of ordinary people and everyday life. Women, African-Americans and other ethnic groups, children, and working class men and women are now studied in great detail. While authority and empowerment remain as subjects of great interest, new historians are much more interested in the ways in which gender, class, and race themselves become agents of social change.

Thirdly, new historians have been influenced by the work of social scientists. Members of the French *Annales* school introduced the study of *mentalité*, a word to describe a panoramic view of history that encompasses geography, economics, demography, social structures, plus mental states, emotions, values, and goals.[19] Historians using this approach to the study of history also often cite the influence of anthropologists such as Mary Douglas, Victor Turner, and particularly Clifford Geertz, who coined the phrase "thick description" to advocate an approach to the study of culture that attempted to reconstruct layers of meaning in social interactions.[20] New historians following these models, including Rhys Isaacs, Lawrence Levine, and Carroll Smith-Rosenberg, study changes occurring over time, often involving nonliterary individuals or groups as agents of change, and are concerned with the context in which these changes came about.[21]

Finally, not only the subjects of history have changed, but the historians view of history and themselves has been radically altered. From the 1950s through the 1960s American historians such as Daniel Boorstin, and Arthur Schlesinger, Jr. strove to preserve a version of history that is described as "consensus history".[22] The Cold War was a significant incentive for them to want to protect America's cultural and national identity and values. They assumed that all Americans shared the same values, and thus they ignored or played down the ideological, social, gender, racial, or class conflicts that occurred throughout America's past. During the 1960's young historians began to focus on multicultural aspects of American history and paid particular attention to issues relating to conflict and/or change.[23]

All of these changes had an influence on libraries and archives as historians began to expand the universe of evidence they would consider. Librarians found that women's diaries, for example, were in greater use than statesmen's papers. Yet while these changes were going on, very little changed in terms of attitudes towards images. The traditional hierarchy of written texts—archives, manuscripts, and imprints, in that order—was being replaced by a new non-hierarchical pool of evidence that included quantifiable data such as census, insurance, and tax statistics but which still placed texts over images. The young scholars whose work ushered in the new social history during the 1960's and 1970's—Stephan Thernstrom, Eugene Genovese, Howard Zinn, Herbert Gutman, Aileen Kraditor, and Eric Foner, among others—did not include images in their books.[24] While the subjects they chose to write about and their interpretations were radically different from that of earlier historians, such as Oscar Handlin, Daniel Boorstin, Arthur Schlesinger, Jr. and Samuel Eliot Morison, the younger historians were not radically departing from a reliance on the same sources as the earlier historians—written or textual evidence. Sophisticated selection and analysis of visual images in scholarly history publications is a fairly recent phenomenon, evolving through the influence of other academic fields.

THE EVOLUTION OF THE USE OF IMAGES

When images do appear in scholarly history books their use can be categorized in three ways: as illustrations, as the means for interpretation, and in a few cases as the means for illumination.[25] Each of these approaches demonstrates the range in historians' "comfort level" with images. For the purposes of this paper, I have limited myself to scholarly publications dealing with nineteenth century American history because I am particularly interested in the visual environment of the nineteenth century.

For the category "images as illustrations" I have selected two publications to discuss: Alan Trachtenberg's *Brooklyn Bridge: Fact and Symbol* (New York: Oxford University Press, 1965) and Sean Wilentz's *Chants Democratic: New York City and the Rise of the American Working Class, 1788–1850* (New York: Oxford University Press, 1984). Trachtenberg's book attracted me because he includes a broad range of texts and images in a classic American Studies approach, exploring what the Brooklyn Bridge meant to Americans when it was created and what it has come to represent in terms of American character and values. He sees the bridge as an American cultural symbol, so I assumed that his choice of images was made as carefully as his choice of words for the chapter headings: "Wilderness Transformed", "The Rainbow and the Grid", "An American Dream", "A Monument", "The Shadow of a Myth". Unfortunately, Trachtenberg did not incorporate into his discussion all the images that he included in the book. How frustrating to have John Marin's and Joseph Stella's paintings reproduced and interpreted, when other paintings are reproduced and not even mentioned. It would seem that the author was intrigued with these paintings and simply included them in his book to share—but not explain—his enjoyment of them with his readers. Trachtenberg's images thus illustrates the book for the most part, in a way that ultimately frustrated me. I wanted to prefer Trachtenberg's study of the bridge over David McCullough's approach to the subject. McCullough's *The Great Bridge* (New York: Simon and Schuster, 1972) is addressed to a popular audience of history buffs who are interested in the bridge as a technological feat (i.e. the great event of traditional history). The subtitle reads *The Epic Story of the Building of the Brooklyn Bridge* and the book jacket describes the book in breathless prose:

> This monumental book brings back for American readers the heroic vision of the America we once had. It is the completely enthralling story of the very greatest event in our nation's history at the time when we were living in the Age of Optimism—a period when Americans were convinced in their hearts that all things were not only possible to accomplish but that they were *good* things of which to be proud.

Setting aside the fact that McCullough's book is an example of the old-fashioned, but still popular history-speaking-for-itself approach, it remains a "good read" with loads of entertainment value, and as such his use of images as illustrations is straightforward and enjoyable. The reader is not left wondering why certain images were included. It's obvious that McCullough anticipated the reader's curiosity about how the bridge was built and about the men who built it. The pictures and captions give you loads of visual information. But with no attempt to interpret the intent of the image makers, the effect of the images on contemporary viewers, or the ways in which the images themselves relate to the culture of the time, McCullough's book demonstrates a simplistic approach to images as historical evidence.

Sean Wilentz's book *Chants Democratic* includes twenty-one images relating to labor and the working class. Almost all are woodcuts, wood engravings, or lithographs, i.e., inexpensive formats that could have been widely disseminated. These images offer enormous interpretive potential as historical evidence relating to wide-spread working-class culture. Wilentz is intrigued enough by them to include them in his book, but his captions and references in the text to the images are kept to a minimum. For example, in his chapter "Artisan Republicanism" he discusses artisan parades, describing each occupational group carrying banners that indicated the trade represented. Yet he passes up the opportunity to interpret what the banners represented in terms of working class values and cohesion, and to analyze the impact of parades and banners on the participants and the parade's viewers. In another part of the book he illustrates trade emblems for early nineteenth-century house painters and chair makers that might have decorated the banners, but his minimal caption informs the reader that what one is seeing is "a kaleidoscope of artisan republican iconography"[26] without defining iconography or explaining what emblems meant to contemporary viewers. His only mention of the chair makers' emblem in the text is to point out the eagle on the back of the depicted chair. Wilentz relies mostly on written evidence, and doesn't embrace such opportunities to extend his discussion of the development of the working class into the arena of the visual environment. In both Trachtenberg's and Wilentz's books the images were not really necessary to convey the author's interpretation.

For the second category, images used as a means for interpretation, I want to look at Karen Halttunen's *Confidence Men and Painted Women: A Study in Middle-Class Culture in America, 1830–1870* (New Haven: Yale University Press, 1982) and Stuart M. Blumin's *The Emergence of the Middle Class: Social Experience in the American City, 1760–1900* (New York: Cambridge University Press, 1989). In both books the images are essential for the effectiveness of the authors' arguments. Halttunen is interested in how members of the middle class defined themselves and differentiate themselves from members of other classes. Her focus is on sincerity and its outward manifestations in dress, etiquette, and mourning rituals as a means of indicating class identity. Using the traditional art historical "compare and contrast" method to make a point, she uses fashion plates to demonstrate how changes that manifested themselves in dress and decorum were a sign of the increased concern for sincerity. She pairs a fashion plate from 1831 with a plate from 1850, noting in the former "the general air of fussy affectation" in the lines and decoration of the dress, and contrasting that with the later plate, noting in the caption that "the sincere ideal is captured here in the women's drooping posture, their expressions of yearning, and the sentimental caption 'Will he never come.' "[27] Halttunen is to be applauded for using fashion plates as historical evidence. Only recently has the study of taste, fashion, and consumerism been taken seriously by academic scholars. Fashion plates carry as much weight in her arguments about sincerity as the etiquette books she also uses as evidence. While one could argue that fashion plates, like etiquette books, are not reliable evidence of actual behavior or dress, Halttunen wisely selected these images and texts as indicators of cultural values, signs of how people wanted to think of themselves even if they are not always an accurate record of how people actually behave.

Stuart Blumin's study of the emergence of a middle class in the nineteenth century also relies on images to carry significant weight in his argument. He is interested in work and home environments as arenas for the formation of class identity. Most of his images are drawn from commercial sources—views of interiors and exteriors of shops and stores that were published by the manufacturers or shopkeepers in an effort to promote business. As such, these images fall into the same category as Halttunen's fashion plates, a genre of idealized images that historians are only beginning to tap to get at social values. What interests Blumin are developments in store interiors that articulate how retailers, store managers, and salesclerks define themselves and differentiate themselves from the people who actually make what is being sold. Both Blumin and Halttunen rely on the visual information in images to support their arguments, and both authors specifically tell the viewer how to look at the image and what elements to look for. Both authors view images as tools, as building blocks to construct their arguments.

Before moving on to the third category, images as illumination, I want to examine an astonishing illustrated history book by an academic historian that strikes at the heart of the objectivity debate as it relates to images. Michael Lesy's *Wisconsin Death Trip* (New York: Pantheon, 1973) like Marshall McLuhan's *The Medium is the Message* (New York: Random House, 1967) became a popular cult book on college campuses almost from the moment it appeared. It aroused heated responses from scholars. Lesy's book is an album of images which Lesy selected from a collection of over 30,000 glass negatives depicting small town life between 1890 and 1910 taken by Charles Van Schaick, a photographer in Black River Falls, Wisconsin. Lesy's scholarly interest lies in "the underworld" of America's collective psyche. Interspersed with the photographs of ordinary folks in Black River Falls are short unrelated excerpts drawn from the local newspaper recounting insanity, suicides, murders, illness, bizarre behavior, superstition, mutilation of animals, and various other forms of sad and desperate behavior. "Lesy offers us a unique opportunity to face not the American Dream, but the American Nightmare ..."[28] For many reviewers, Lesy's book was very disturbing; one reviewer described it as "... one of the most depressing, joyless books I have ever read," and "... a relentless catalogue of human misery."[29] A reviewer in *The New York Times* was more favorable, noting that "The result is an impressive example of the poetry of history ..." [which] "has enlarged on the uses of history,"[30] but other reviewers could not restrain their outrage about Lesy's reading of the images. It was described as "an exercise in manipulation" by Gerald Weales, a professor of English at the University of Pennsylvania. Professor Weales' review tells us as much about how historians view images as it does about Lesy's book.

> In an attempt to make the pictures *mean* in a way in which they were never intended—nor would now if presented directly—Lesy goes in for a variety of tricks. His juxtapositions—live babies alongside coffined babies is the most obvious—are meant to surprise us into new perceptions, I assume but they seem simply artificial editorializing, although perhaps not quite as annoying as the games he plays when he

doctors photographs. He frequently presents the same photograph twice ... He occasionally draws a large black circle around one figure in a group and he is fond of enlarging individual faces taken from group photographs, perhaps as a means of emphasizing the kind of dementedly staring quality that is the inevitable result—check your own school pictures—of an uneasy subject meeting an indifferent photographer ... Lesy, then, forces himself between me and the pictures ...[31]

There are several interesting aspects of this quotation: Weales feels that photographs speak for themselves, that if they were "presented directly" they would convey an intended message. In Weales' mind the images are transparent, enabling the viewer to see the past, so long as the person presenting the image does not "force himself" between the image and the viewer.

If Lesy had described himself as an artist, and described his book as a photo essay, it would have likely been reviewed in a far different way. When an artist or photographer like Diane Arbus produces a collection of images that reflects a negative point of view towards life in America, critics expect a subjective element in the work. In his preface to *Wisconsin Death Trip* Warren Susman drew a comparison between Lesy's approach and Hannah Arendt's description of Walter Benjamin's method of creating a "surrealistic montage."[32] Lesy's use of images resembles the postmodernist practice of appropriation common to photographers such as Richard Prince, who photographs pictures in magazines, cropping and arranging them in ways similar to Lesy.[33] When it was published, only the photographer and novelist Wright Morris recognized that *Wisconsin Death Trip* was a departure from mainstream historical writing. "Mr. Lesy", Morris wrote in the *New York Times*, "projects a world that is best judged on its own merits, as we would judge a novel or a collage."[34] More recently, the historian Simon Schama in *Dead Certainties: (Unwarranted Speculations)* (New York: Knopf, 1991) has taken similar liberties with historical evidence, but with the passage of time readers are accustomed to (or at least somewhat more comfortable with) this post-modernist presentation of history. Schama himself describes the book as "a work of the imagination that chronicles historical events", in this case the heroic death of General James Wolfe in 1759 and the mysterious death of George Parkman in 1849.

> Though these stories may at times appear to observe the discursive conventions of history, they are in fact historical novellas since some passages ... are pure inventions, based, however, on what documents suggest. This is not to say, I should emphasize, that I scorn the boundary between fact and fiction. It is merely to imply that even in the most austere scholarly report from the archives, the inventive faculty—selecting, pruning, editing, commenting, interpreting, delivering judgments—is in full play.[35]

Lesy, like Schama, was unfazed as a historian with his own inventive faculty in full play. A recent overview of Lesy's oeuvre called it a form of voyeurism, and provided an excellent criteria for evaluating the use of images. Do the images require the viewer to make connections, to ponder meanings, even when they are multiple or ambiguous?[36]

That way of looking—making connections, pondering meanings—is indeed what I had in mind when we turn to my last category, image as illumination. The work of very few academic historians fall into this category. Two that should definitely be included are Warren Susman and Michael Kammen. Both scholars are particularly sensitive to the way images relate to American memory, tradition, and national identity. Kammen and Susman utilize images as evidence, but they have also at times achieved something rare: they illuminate the meaning of the images and what is being depicted in a way that changes how we view our world from that moment on. Here are some examples. In *Culture as History: The Transformation of American Society in the Twentieth Century* (New York: Pantheon, 1984) Warren Susman purposely states that "the consumption of images is basic to an understanding of the culture ...."[37] He intersperses his chapters with six pairs of images unrelated to the text. His juxtaposed images are devoted to the themes of George Washington, skyscrapers, food, the American flag, the urban scene, and religion. His choices are attempts to demonstrate contrasts between differing attitudes, differing lifestyles, or between ideals and reality. They are not profound choices—the pair of images relating to the American flag are the raising of the flag after the battle of Iwo Jima and a film still from *Easy Rider* showing the actor Peter Fonda in a motorcycle helmet and leather jacket decorated with the American flag.

Yet such seemingly simple juxtapositions are often the most provocative. Kammen's use of images is also seemingly simplistic on one level. In *A Season of Youth: the American Revolution and the Historical Imagination* (New York: Knopf, 1978) he describes the change from a revolutionary culture to a republican culture by discussing the proliferation of images showing eagles and the figure of Liberty during the revolution, and the proliferation of images which include plows and cornucopias after the revolution. The effect he achieves will influence readers long after they put down Kammen's book. There is the experience of discovery, of experiencing a sense of "Ah-Ha!", of heightened consciousness. Kammen has changed how the reader relates to these images and how the reader thinks about history. Art historians might not be so impressed, as the iconography of the eagle and the cornucopia is well documented in art literature. Yet this apparently simple coupling of eagles and Liberty with plows and cornucopias to make a point about historical change is very effective.

Kammen's more recent publications demonstrate his intense interest in visual manifestations of memory and how versions of the past are created or perpetuated.[38] These books are of singular importance for anyone interesting in exploring the relationship between visual images and history, and how Americans create, remember, and celebrate memories of the past.

MODELS FROM OTHER ACADEMIC FIELDS

Historians seeking methodological models for the use of images as historical evidence may find it useful to examine recent literature in the fields of anthropology, media studies, art history, material culture studies and consumerism, popular culture, literary studies, and cultural studies. (See Appendix) In particular, reader-response theory may suggest ways that historians can approach images as evidence. Certain art and literary historians share an interest in analyzing a work of art—literary or visual in format—from the point of view of the reader or viewer. "Reader-response critics would argue that a poem cannot be understood apart from its results". Its "effects," psychological and otherwise, are essential to any accurate description of its meaning, since that meaning has no effective existence outside of its realization in the mind of a reader.[39]

An exciting recent publication concerned with viewer response is David Freedberg's book, *The Power of Images: Studies in the History and Theory of Response* (University of Chicago Press, 1993). It focuses on the relationship between images and viewers, particularly the psychological and behavioral responses to images. Most of the images he examines are outside the mainstream of high style art; in fact they might not be considered art by certain art historians. The funeral effigies, pornographic images, wax figures, billboards, and posters, elicit responses that could be described as irrational, superstitious, primitive, and occasionally embarrassing to Western intellectuals. However, by concentrating on what might be considered unconscious or superstitious responses he demonstrates the enormously powerful effect of images outside of or in addition to the effect the modern/ intellectual viewer associates with all kinds of images. By focusing attention on the powerful effect images can have on their viewers, Freedberg and the other "viewer response" theorists elevate the status of images as evidence, and thus offer historians a compelling reason for considering images to be as effective as written evidence in the writing of history.

On the other hand, by highlighting the response and the fact that multifaceted and often unconscious responses can occur, viewer-response theory can intimidate historians who may not be completely comfortable using images whose effect they cannot predict, comprehend, or control. Images, like literary texts, are subject to numerous interpretations. This fact only serves to remind historians that they exist in the postmodern age—wherein the debate (performance) is often more important than the event or object being interpreted. It's not an easy time to be a historian.

CONCLUSION: HISTORY AS AN ARTIFACT

Ultimately, regardless of methodological approach, when historians select and arrange images in a book, they are creating an artifact, a visual entity with a set of characteristics that can exist apart from the text of the book, while simultaneously enhancing the text of the book. An arrangement of images causes the viewer to draw connections between and among the images, expanding on the meaning the images can have individually. And when texts and images are skillfully intertwined in the layout of the book, a synergy exists between them that produces an effect in the reader/viewer beyond what the text or the images can do without the other. Today, both academic and non-academic readers are growing highly receptive to information in numerous varieties, including visual images. While postmodernism may have set scholars adrift, it has also presented them with the freedom that flux allows: information can be created, packaged, transmitted and experienced in a myriad of ways. Images read singly or in narrative sequence, moving or frozen, have enormous possibilities in helping us order our world and explain the past. As more than one historian has pointed out, images are often more potent than texts in conveying a sense of history.

> ...a print [engraving] is not a treatise; its direct impact is never so much on our reason as on our emotions and passions. But the motion and excitement conveyed may well serve as valuable means to the end of understanding. Both the 'distortion' and the enchantment of art may often penetrate to the essence of an event more keenly than either 'factual' accounts or rational discourse. It is in this way that art, which at first might seem inferior to both history and reason, may, on the level of actual insight, surpass them both.[40]

Furthermore, if academic historians avoid images in their research are they running the risk that their modes of intellectual inquiries could be defined by the kinds of documents or evidence to which they restrict themselves? In other words, are they missing out on all sorts of opportunities for expanding the range of their questions if they ignore pictorial documents in favor of written documents? According to Alan Trachtenberg, the fact that photographs can be interpreted so many ways "... frees us from the tyranny of any fixed version [of history], permitting critical historical judgment."[41] Historians who use images as evidence may do so with a feeling that the ground is moving under their feet. But if those academic historians who prefer texts avoid acknowledging the public's growing visual literacy and sophistication they run the risk of making themselves obsolete.

APPENDIX: MODELS FOR THE USE OF IMAGES AS EVIDENCE

TEXTBOOKS

I have purposely avoided discussing textbooks in this article, in part because they deserve far more attention than space allows. Textbooks are a complex issue because they are not considered important within academia, i.e. not often considered as part of the tenure process; they are written under contract with commercial publishers who have a great deal to say about the finished product; and the audience are non-specialists and are not selecting the books themselves. It is important to note, however, that textbooks do comprise the largest body of illustrated books within the genre of illustrated scholarly history books.

This caveat aside, I will mention and recommend one example for the historian interested in exploring ways to use images as evidence. *Who Built America?* is both a two-volume textbook and an interactive compact disc, the result of a project that began in 1982 under the leadership of historian Herbert Gutman whose goal was to brook the gap between developments in social history research and writing in academia and what the public was getting in popular history. The American Social History Project has as its goal to produce a range of educational products covering U.S. history from 1607 to the end of World War I for students and educators. The textbook and CD-ROM are noteworthy for the weight given to images. Yet while the project staff were clearly committed to producing a visually-oriented body of education material, they remained uneasy about images and their effect on the viewer.

> The visual record of the past—particularly regarding the lives of working men and women, immigrants, and people of color—requires careful consideration ... Pictures that were produced and viewed in specific historical eras can teach us a lot about working peoples' lives, but it is equally important to understand there is much that these pictures obscure or fail to show.[42]

The compact disc version of *Who Built America?* was produced by the Voyager Company (Santa Monica, CA) in 1993 and is accompanied by a 20 page users guide.

ANTHROPOLOGY

In anthropological field work the camera has become an essential tool, and the literature on visual anthropology is extensive. A highly selective list of the major writings that would be of particular pertinence to historians includes the following:

John Collier Jr. and Malcolm Collier, *Visual Anthropology: Photography as a Research Method* (Albuquerque: University of New Mexico Press, 1986).

Sol Worth, *Studying Visual Communication* (Philadelphia: University of Pennsylvania Press, 1981).

Melissa Banta and Curtis Hinsley, *From Site to Sight: Anthropology, Photography and the Power of Imagery* (Cambridge: Peabody Museum Press, 1986).

Anthropology and Photography, 1860–1920, edited by Elizabeth Edwards (New Haven: Yale University Press, 1992)

Joanna Cohan Scherer, "Historical Photographs as Anthropological Documents: A Retrospect," *Visual Anthropology* 3 (1990), pp. 131–155.

Images of Information: Still Photography in the Social Sciences, edited by Jon Wagner (Beverly Hills: Sage, 1979).

Johanna Cohan Scherer, "You Can't Believe Your Eyes: Inaccuracies in Photographs of North American Indians," *Studies in the Anthropology of Visual Communication* 2 (Fall 1975), pp.67–79.

Lonna M. Malmsheimer, "Photographic Analysis as Ethnohistory: Interpretive Strategies," *Visual Anthropology* 1 (1987), pp. 21–36.

David Nye, *Image Worlds: Corporate Identities at General Electric, 1890–1930* (Cambridge: MIT Press, 1985).

The Society for Visual Anthropology, established in 1973, is a unit of the American Anthropological Association whose members are interested in the use of visual images in anthropological research, teaching, and writing. The Society's publications offer some of the best theoretical and practical models for the use of images as evidence.[43] The Graduate Association of Visual Anthropologists at Temple University sponsors an electronic discussion group, VISCOM, devoted to the study of culture and visual communication and teaching with media.[44]

PHOTOGRAPHY AND FILM

There are an increasing number of historians who study images, including documentary photography, advertisements and documentary and commercial films, as cultural and social indicators.

I. Theory

John Tagg, *The Burden of Representation: Essays on Photographies and Histories* (Minneapolis: University of Minnesota Press, 1988).

Alan Trachtenberg, *Reading American Photographs: Images as History, Mathew Brady to Walker Evans* (New York: Hill and Wang, 1989).

Alan Trachtenberg, "Photographs as Symbolic History," in *The American Image: Photographs from the National Archives, 1860–1960* (New York: Pantheon Books, 1979).

John E. O'Connor, *Image as Artifact: The Historical Analysis of Film and Television* (Malabar: Robert E. Krieger Publishing Co. for the American Historical Association, 1990).

Robert M. Levine, *Images of History: Nineteenth and Early Twentieth Century Latin American Photographs as Documents* (Durham: Duke University Press, 1989).

Erving Goffman, *Gender Advertisements* (New York: Harper and Row, 1979).

II. Models

Lawrence Levine, "The Historian and the Icon: Photography and the History of the American People in the 1930s and 1940s," in *Documenting America, 1935–1943*, edited by Carl Fleischhauer and Beverly W. Brannan (Berkeley: University of California Press, 1988), pp. 15–42.

Alan Trachtenberg, "From Image to Story: Reading the File," in *Documenting America, 1935–1943*, edited by Carl Fleischhauer and Beverly W. Brannan (Berkeley: University of California Press, 1988), pp. 43–73.

James Curtis, *Mind's Eye, Mind's Truth: FSA Photography Reconsidered* (Philadelphia: Temple University Press, 1989).

William Stott, *Documentary Expression and Thirties America* (New York: Oxford University Press, 1973).

F. Jack Hurley, *Portrait of a Decade: Roy Stryker and the Development of Documentary Photography in the Thirties* (Baton Rouge: Louisiana State University Press, 1972).

Maren Stange, *Symbols of Ideal Life: Social Documentary Photography in America, 1890–1950* (New York: Cambridge University Press, 1989).

Susan Moeller, *Shooting War: Photography and the American Experience of Combat* (New York: Basic Books, 1989).

Richard E. Jensen, et al., *Eyewitness at Wounded Knee* (Lincoln: University of Nebraska Press, 1991).

III. Films, Television and Teaching

Resisting Images: Essays on Cinema and History, edited by Robert Sklar and Charles Musser (Philadelphia: Temple University Press, 1990).

American History/American Film: Interpreting the Hollywood Image, edited by John E. O'Connor and Martin A. Jackson (New York: Ungar, 1988).

American History/American Television: Interpreting the Video Past, edited by John E. O'Connor (New York: Ungar, 1988).

Hollywood As Historian: American Film in a Cultural Context edited by Peter C. Rollins (Lexington, University Press of Kentucky, 1983).

"Popular Films and Historical Memory," in *Learning History in America: Schools, Cultures, and Politics*, edited by Lloyd Kramer, et al. (Minnesota: University of Minnesota Press, 1994).

Sessions devoted to media and history are regularly held at the annual professional meetings of historians: the American Historical Association, the Organization of American Historians, and the American Studies Association, for example; films are reviewed in *The Journal of American History*; *The American Historical Review*, and *Radical History Review*; and there is even a journal *Film and History*, devoted to the topic.[45] For several years the Organization of American Historians has awarded a history film prize (the Erik Barnouw Award), and in 1993 the American Historical Association inaugurated the John E. O'Connor Award, given to films or videos dealing with history. Recently an electronic discussion group, H-Film, devoted to "the scholarly studies and uses of media", was established within the network of electronic history discussion groups sponsored by the History Department at the University of Illinois.[46] In April 1993 a three-day conference entitled "Telling the Story: The Media, the Public and American History" organized by the New England Foundation for the Humanities attracted over 800 attendees who hotly debated the merits of films such as Ken Burns' *Civil War* and were ultimately frustrated by differences over the objectivity issue and by the participants' multiple definitions of history.[47]

ART HISTORY AND POPULAR VISUAL CULTURE

Art historians have traditionally shared with historians a concern for the provenance of their evidence: while historians are concerned with the genuineness of documents, art historians are trained to recognize fake works of art. In recent years, many art historians have moved beyond connoisseurship: from being 'object-centered' they are increasingly becoming 'object-driven'.[48] Many of the authors cited below study works of art in a contextual fashion, or have become cultural historians using images as their principle evidence to support an historical argument.

I. Method and Theory

Rudolf Arnheim, *Visual Thinking* (Berkeley: University of California Press, 1969).

E. H. Gombrich, *Art and Illusion: A Study in the Psychology of Pictorial Representation* (Princeton: Princeton University Press, 1961).

Norman Bryson, *Visual Culture: Images and Interpretations* (University Press of New England, 1994)

Norman Bryson, ed., *Visual Theory: Painting and Interpretation* (London: Polity Press, 1991).

W. J. T. Mitchell, *Iconology: Image, Text, Ideology* (Chicago: University of Chicago Press, 1986).

W. J. T. Mitchell, *Picture Theory: Essays on Verbal and Visual Representation* (Chicago: University of Chicago Press, 1994).

Stuart Ewan, *All Consuming Images: The Politics of Style in Contemporary Culture* (New York: Basic Books, 1988).

"The Evidence of Art: Images and Meaning in History," *The Journal of Interdisciplinary History* (Summer 1986), Issue.

David Freedberg and Jan de Vries, eds. *Art in History/History in Art: Studies in Seventeenth-Century Dutch Culture* (Malibu: Getty Center for the History of Arts and the Humanities, 1991).

Francis Haskell, *History and its Images: Art and the Interpretation of the Past* (New Haven: Yale University Press, 1993).

Irving Lavin. *Past–Present: Essays on Historicism in Art from Donatello to Picasso* (Berkeley: University of California Press, 1993).

Stephen Bann. *The Clothing of Clio: A Study of the Representation of History in Nineteenth-Century Britain and France* (Cambridge: Cambridge University Press, 1984).

Stephen Bann. *The Inventions of History: Essays on the Representation of the Past* (Manchester: Manchester University Press, 1990).

II. Models

Sarah Burns, *Pastoral Inventions: Rural Life in Nineteenth-Century American Art and Culture* (Philadelphia: Temple University Press, 1989).

Michele Bogart, *Public Sculpture and the Civic Ideal in New York City, 1890–1930* (Chicago: University of Chicago Press, 1989).

Elizabeth Johns, *American Genre Painting: the Politics of Everyday Life* (New Haven: Yale University Press, 1991).

Elizabeth Johns, *Thomas Eakins: The Heroism of Modern Life* (Princeton: Princeton University Press, 1983).

Alan Wallach and William Truettner, eds., *Thomas Cole: Landscape Into History* (New Haven: Yale University Press, 1994).

Albert Boime, *The Art of Exclusion: Representing Blacks in the Nineteenth Century* (Washington: Smithsonian Institution Press, 1990).

Ellen Wiley Todd, *The 'New Woman' Revised: Painting and Gender Politics on Fourteenth Street* (Berkeley: University of California Press, 1993).

Martha Banta. *Imagining American Women: Idea and Ideals in Cultural History* (New York: Columbia University Press, 1987).

Alice Sheppard, *Cartooning for Suffrage* (Albuquerque: University of New Mexico Press, 1994).

Dick Hebdige, *Hiding in the Light: On Images and Things* (New York: Routledge, 1988).

Joseph Witek, *Comic Books as History: The Narrative Art of Jack Jackson, Art Spiegelman, and Harvey Pekar* (Jackson, University Press of Mississippi, 1989).

Petra Chu and Gabriel Weisberg, eds. *The Popularization of Images: Visual Culture under the July Monarchy.* (Princeton: Princeton University Press, 1994).

Peter Paret, *Art as History: Essays in the Culture and Politics of Nineteenth-Century Germany* (Princeton: Princeton University Press, 1988).

Jan Bremmer and Herman Roodenburg, eds., *A Cultural History of Gesture* (Ithaca: Cornell University Press, 1991).

III. Art Exhibitions

Several recent exhibition resulting from collaborative efforts between historians and art historians include:

William Truettner, *The West as America: Reinterpreting Images of the Frontier, 1820–1920* (Washington: Smithsonian Institution Press, 1991).

Jules Prown, *Discovered Lands, Invented Pasts: Transforming Visions of the American West* (New Haven: Yale University Press, 1992).

Giu McElroy, *Facing History: The Black Image in American Art, 1710–1940*, (Washington: Corcoran Gallery of Art, 1990).

Alfred F. Young and Terry J. Fife, *We the People: Voices and Images of the New Nation*, (Philadelphia: Temple University Press for the Chicago Historical Society, 1993).

Eric Foner and Olivia Mahoney, *A House Divided: America in the Age of Lincoln* (New York: W. W. Norton & Co. for the Chicago Historical Society, 1990).

William Ayres, ed., *Picturing History: American Painting 1770–1930* (New York: Rizzoli for Fraunces Tavern Museum, 1993).

Philip S. Foner, *The Other America: Art and the Labour Movement in the United States* (London: Journeyman Press, 1985).

MATERIAL CULTURE AND CONSUMERISM

These fields offer the historian the largest body of literature as models for using non-textual and non-verbal records as evidence. The titles listed below offer methodological and theoretical approaches, plus application models. While the list below is brief, I recommend the footnotes and bibliographies in each of the works cited.

Thomas J. Schlereth, "Material Culture Studies in America, 1876–1976," in *Material Culture Studies in America*, edited by Thomas J. Schlereth (Nashville: American Association for State and Local History, 1982), pp. 1–78.

Christopher Tilley, ed., *Reading Material Culture: Structuralism, Hermeneutics, and Post-Structuralism* (New York: Basil Blackwell, 1988).

Ann Smart Martin, "Makers, Buyers, and Users: Consumerism as a Material Culture Framework," *Winterthur Portfolio*, 28 (Summer/Autumn 1993), pp. 141–157.

Grant McCracken, *Culture and Consumption: New Approaches to the Symbolic Character of Consumer Goods and Activities* (Bloomington: Indiana University Press, 1988).

Robert Blair St. George, ed., *Material Life in America, 1600–1860* (Boston: Northeastern University Press, 1988).

Steven Lubar and W. David Kingery, *History from Things: Essays on Material Culture* (Washington: Smithsonian Institution Press, 1993).

Gerald L. Pocius, ed., *Living in a Material World: Canadian and American Approaches to Material Culture*, (Social and Economics Papers: no. 19) (St. John's, Memorial University of Newfoundland, Institute of Social and Economic Research, 1991).

Grier, Katherine C., *Culture and Comfort: People, Parlors, and Upholstery, 1850–1930* (Rochester, N.Y.: Strong Museum, 1988).

CULTURAL STUDIES

Cultural Studies is a growing area of academic interest, attracting scholars interested in the culture of gender, class, and ethnicity in relation to social, political, and ideological hegemony, and focus on the active (not passive) role of consumers in relation to contemporary mass culture. This interdisciplinary field got its start in England, at the University of Birmingham's Centre for Contemporary Cultural Studies established in 1968, with the work of Raymond Williams and Stuart Hall having perhaps the greatest influence in shaping the field's evolving self-definition. Three examples drawn from the literature of Cultural Studies that demonstrate methods for analyzing visual representations are

Catherine A. Lutz and Jane L. Collins, *Reading National Geographic* (Chicago: University of Chicago Press, 1993).

Jan Nederveen Pieterse, *White on Black: Images of Africa and Blacks in Western Popular Culture* (New Haven: Yale University Press, 1992).

"Work and Consumption in Visual Representations" in *Gender and American History Since 1890*, edited by Barbara Melosh (London: Routledge, 1992).

NOTES

1. J. H. Huizinga, "My Path to History," in his *Dutch Civilization in the Seventeenth Century and Other Essays* (New York: F. Unger, 1968), p. 269, quoted in Michael Kamman, *A Season of Youth: The American Revolution and the Historical Imagination* (New York: Knopf, 1978), p. 77.

2. One could argue that textbooks are the demilitarized zone between popular history and scholarly history, because the writers are generally historians and the audience is usually nonspecialists. I have purposely avoided talking about textbooks although they comprise the largest body of illustrated academic history books. See the paragraph at the beginning of the appendix.

3. Readers may also wish to examine the following: "Mirrors of the Past: Historical Photography and American History," in Thomas J. Schlereth, *Artifacts and the American Past* (Nashville: American Association for State and Local History, 1980); Marsha Peters and Bernard Mergen, " 'Doing the Rest': The Uses of Photographs in American Studies," *American Quarterly* 29, no. 3 (1977), p. 281; James Borchert, "Analysis of Historical Photographs: A Method and a Case Study," *Studies in Visual Communication* 7 (Fall 1981), pp. 30–67; George W. Dowdall and Janet Golden, "Photographs as Data: An Analysis of Images from a Mental Hospital," *Qualitative Sociology* 12 (Summer 1989), pp. 183–213; Eric Margolis,

"Mining Photographs: Unearthing the Meanings of Historical Photos," *Radical History Review* 40 (1988), pp. 33–48.

4. Jon Wagner, *Images of Information: Still Photography in the Social Sciences* (Beverly Hills: Sage, 1979), p. 265. An excellent discussion of this dichotomy as it occurs in historiography is Georg G. Iggers, "Historical Methodologies and Research," in *Teaching Bibliographic Skills in History: A Sourcebook for Historians and Librarians* (Westport: Greenwood Press, 1993), pp. 3–24.

5. John Collier, Jr. and Malcolm Collier, *Visual Anthropology: Photography as a Research Method* (Albuquerque: University of New Mexico Press, 1986), pp. 169–170. This attitude towards texts and images is clearly applied in John Agresto, "Art and Historical Truth: the Boston Massacre," in *Journal of Communication* 29 (1979), pp. 170–174, wherein the author claims that "What actually took place [based on his readings of historical texts] ... bears little resemblance to the image of it that [Paul] Revere's print has since engraved on the American mind." (p. 170).

6. Karin J. MacHardy, "Crises in History, or: Hermes Unbounded," *Storia della Storiografia* 17 (1990, p. 24).

7. *The Literature of American History: A Bibliographic Guide*, edited by J. N. Larned (Boston: Houghton Mifflin & Co. for the American Library Association, 1902).

8. For example, no mention is made of picture collections and the use of images as historical evidence in Walter Rundell, Jr., *In Pursuit of American History: Research and Training in the United States* (Norman: University of Oklahoma Press, 1970); Charles A. D'Aniello, ed., *Teaching Bibliographic Skills in History: A Sourcebook for Historians and Librarians* (Westport: Greenwood Press, 1993); Thomas P. Slavens, *Sources of Information for Historical Research* (New York: Neal-Schuman, 1994); or Ron Blazek and Anna H. Perrault, *United States History: A Selective Guide to Information Sources* (Englewood: Libraries Unlimited, 1994).

9. Irwin Unger, "The 'New Left' and American History: Some Recent Trends in United States Historiography," *American Historical Review* 72 (July 1967), p. 1263.

10. *Harvard Guide to American History*, ed. by Frank Freidel (Cambridge: Harvard University Press, 1974), p. 50. Freidel did not feel compelled to update the caveat about images given to readers in the *Guide*'s first edition in 1954. One might view this inclusion of a section on pictorial records as a step forward, however. The precursor to the 1954 *Harvard Guide* was *Guide to the Study and Reading of American History* by three Harvard historians, Edward Channing, Albert Bushnell Hart, and Frederick Jackson Turner, in 1896. Neither this edition nor the 1912 revision included any mention of picture collections or discuss the use of images as historical evidence.

11. *New Perspectives on Historical Writing*, edited by Peter Burke (University Park: Pennsylvania State University Press, 1992).

12. Michiko Kakutani, "Fiction? Nonfiction? And Why Doesn't Anybody Care?" *New York Times*, July 27, 1993, p. B8.

13. On White's *Metahistory*, see *History and Theory* 19 (1980), and the review by Michael Ermarth in the *American Historical Review* 80 (1975), pp. 961–963. On Novick's *That Noble Dream*, see James T. Kloppenberg, "Objectivity and Historicism: A Century of American Historical Writing," *American Historical Review* 94 (October 1989), pp. 1011–1030; Thomas L. Haskell, "Objectivity is Not Neutrality: Rhetoric vs. Practice in Peter Novick's 'That Noble Dream,'" *History and Theory* 19 (1990), pp. 129–157; and "Peter Novick's 'That Noble Dream': The Objectivity Question and the Future of the Historical Profession," *American Historical Review* 96 (1991), pp. 675–708, which includes essays by five historians with a rebuttal by Novick.

14. Michiko Kakutani, op. cit., p. B1.

15. Vicki Goldberg, "Remembering the Faces in the Civil Rights Struggle," *New York Times*, July 17, 1994, pp. H31–H32.

16. Digital technology is explained and analyzed in William J. T. Mitchell, "When is Seeing Believing?" *Scientific American* 270 (February 1994), pp. 68–75 and William J. T. Mitchell, *The Reconfigured Eye: Visual Truth in the Post-Photographic Era* (Cambridge: MIT Press, 1992). The controversy concerning a composite photograph on the cover of the newspaper *New York Newsday* of Tonya Harding appearing to skate next to Nancy Kerrigan was discussed in William Glaverson, "*Newsday* Imagines an Event, and Sets Off a Debate," *New York Times*, February 17, 1994, p. D22.

17. The origin and meaning of the phrase "New History" is discussed by Peter Burke, "Overture: the New History, its Past and its Future," in *New Perspectives on Historical Writing*, edited by Peter Burke (University Park: Pennsylvania State University Press), pp. 1–23.

18. *Ibid.*

19. Roger Chartier, "Intellectual History of Sociocultural History? The French Trajectories," in *Modern European Intellectual History: Reappraisals and New Perspectives*, edited by Dominick LaCapra and Steven L. Kaplan (Ithaca: Cornell University Press, 1982); Lynn Hunt; "French History in the Last Twenty Years," *Journal of Contemporary History* 21 (1986), pp. 209–224. For an example of the application by an American historian of the Annales methodology, see James A. Henretta, "Families and Farms: Mentalité in Pre-Industrial America," *William and Mary Quarterly* 35 (1978).

20. Mary Douglas, *Natural Symbols: Explorations in Cosmology* (New York: Pantheon, 1970); Victor Turner, *Dramas, Fields, and Metaphors: Symbolic Action in Human Society* (Ithaca: Cornell University Press, 1974); Clifford Geertz, "Thick Description: Toward an Interpretive Theory of Culture," in his *The Interpretation of Cultures: Selected Essays* (New York: Basic Books, 1973), pp. 3–32. See also, Aletta Biersack, "Local Knowledge, Local History: Geertz and Beyond," in *The New Cultural History*, edited by Lynn Hunt (Berkeley: University of California Press, 1989) and Ronald G. Walters, "Signs of the Times: Clifford Geertz and Historians," *Social Research* 47 (1980), pp. 537–556.

21. Rhys Isaac, *The Transformation of Virginia, 1740–1790* (Chapel Hill: University of North Carolina Press, 1982); Lawrence W. Levine, "Slave Songs and Slave Consciousness: Explorations in Neglected Sources," in his *The Unpredictable Past: Explorations in American Cultural History* (New York: Oxford University Press, 1993); Carroll Smith-Rosenberg, *Disorderly Conduct: Visions of Gender in Victorian America* (New York: Knopf, 1985).

22. Michael Kraus and Davis D. Joyce, "Consensus: American Historical Writing in the 1950s," in their *The Writing of American History* (Norman: University of Oklahoma Press, 1985): 311–335. This approach was criticized by John Higham in "The Cult of the 'American Consensus': Homogenizing Our History," *Commentary* 27 (February 1959), pp. 93–101.

23. Barton J. Bernstein, *Towards a New Past: Dissenting Essays in American History* (New York: Vintage, 1968); Irwin Unger, *Beyond Liberalism: The New Left Views American History* (Toronto: Xerox College Publishing, 1971); *The Past Before Us: Contemporary Historical Writing in the United States*, edited by Michael Kamman (Ithaca: Cornell University Press, 1980); "Conflict: American Historical Writing in the 1960s," in Michael Kraus and Davis D. Joyce, *The Writing of American History* (Norman: University of Oklahoma Press, 1985), pp. 336–368.

24. Stephan Thernstrom, *Poverty and Progress: Social Mobility in a Nineteenth Century City* (Cambridge: Harvard University Press, 1964); Euegene Genovese, *The World the Slaveholders Made* (New York: Pantheon, 1969); Eugene Genovese, *Roll, Jordan, Roll: The World the Slaves Made* (New York: Pantheon, 1974); Howard Zinn, *SNCC: The New Abolitionists* (Boston: Beacon Press, 1964); Herbert Gutman, *Work, Culture, and Society in Industrializing America* (New York: Knopf, 1976); Aileen Kraditor, *Up From the Pedestal: Selected Writings from the History of Feminism* (Chicago: Quadrangle Books, 1968); Eric Foner, *Free Soil, Free Labor, Free Men: The Ideology of the Republican Party* (New York: Oxford University Press, 1970).

25. For discussing this essay through several drafts and for his help and encouragement in developing this conceptual model I wish to thank my husband, James W. Coleman III.

26. Sean Wilentz, *Chants Democratic: New York City and the Rise of the American Working Class, 1788–1850* (New York: Oxford University Press, 1984), figure 6.

27. Karen Halttunen, *Confidence Men and Painted Women: A Study of Middle-Class Culture in America, 1830–1870* (New Haven: Yale University Press 1982), pp. 76–79.

28. Warren Susman, "Preface," in Michael Lesy, *Wisconsin Death Trip* (New York: Pantheon, 1973), n.p.

29. Philip French, "Dear Dead Days," *New Statesman* 86 (November 2, 1973).

30. William H. Gass [book review], *New York Times Book Review*, June 24, 1973, pp. 7, 18.

31. Gerald Weales, "Is This Trip Necessary?" *North American Review* 258 (Fall 1973), pp. 79–80.

32. Hannah Arendt, "Introduction," in Walter Benjamin, *Illuminations*, edited by Hannah Arendt (New York: Harcourt, Brace & World, 1968), pp. 47–48, as quoted by Warren Susman in his preface to Michael Lesy, *Wisconsin Death Trip*, n.p.

33. Andy Grundberg, "The Crisis of the Real: Photography and Postmodernism" in *Multiple Views: Logan Grant Essays on Photography 1983–1989*, edited by Daniel P. Younger (Albuquerque: University of New Mexico Press, 1991), pp. 363–385.

34. Wright Morris, [book review] *New York Times Book Review*, November 28, 1976, p. 2.

35. Simon Schama, *Dead Certainties (Unwarranted Speculations)* (New York: Knopf, 1991), pp. 327, 322.

36. Josh Brown, "Bearing Witness: Michael Lesy and Photography as a Historical Resource," *Film & History* 13 (1983), pp. 43–46.

37. Warren Susman, *Culture as History: The Transformation of American Society in the Twentieth Century* (New York: Pantheon, 1984), p. xvii.

38. *Mystic Chords of Memory: The Transformation of Tradition in American Culture* (New York: Random House, 1991) and *Meadows of Memory: Images of Time and Tradition in American Art and Culture* (Austin: University of Texas Press, 1992).

39. Jane Tompkins, *Reader Response Criticism: From Formalism to Post-Structuralism* (Baltimore: Johns Hopkins University Press, 1980), p. ix. For examples of the application of reader-reponse theory using visual images see the following: Svetlana Alpers, *The Art of Describing: Dutch Art in the Seventeenth Century* (Chicago: University of Chicago Press, 1983); Michael Baxandall, *Patterns of Intention: On the Historical Explanation of Pictures* (New Haven: Yale University Press, 1985); Mieke Bal, *Reading "Rembrandt": Beyond the World-Image Opposition* (Cambridge: Cambridge University Press, 1991); John Berger, *Ways of Seeing* (London: Penguin, 1972).

40. John Agresto, "Art and Historical Truth: The Boston Massacre," in *Journal of Communication* 29 (1979), p. 174. See also the Op-Ed essay about a Robert Capra photograph of D-Day by Alan Trachtenberg, " 'Bullets Tore Holes in the Water'," in *The New York Times*, June 6, 1994, p. A11.

41. Alan Trachtenberg, "From Image to Story: Reading the File," in *Documenting America, 1935–1943*, edited by Carl Fleischhauer and Beverly W. Brannan (Berkeley: University of California Press, 1988), p. 70.

42. American Social History Project, *Who Built America? Working People and the Nation's Economy, Politics, Culture, and Society. Vol. One: From Conquest and Colonization through Reconstruction and the Great Uprising of 1877* (New York: Pantheon, 1989), p. xiv.

43. The Society's jounals include *Studies in Anthropology of Visual Communication* (1974–1979), *Studies in Visual Communication* (1980–1985), and *Society for Visual Anthropology Review* (1985–present). In addition, there is a journal devoted to the subject published in England by Harwood Academic Publishers, entitled *Visual Anthropology* (1987–present).

44. To subscribe to VISCOM send a one-line e-mail message to LISTSERV@VM.TEMPLE.EDU with the message SUBSCRIBE VISCOM and your name.

45. *Film & History* began in 1971, and is published quarterly by the Historians Film Committee at the New Jersey Institute of Technology in Newark, New Jersey. The editor is John E. O'Connor. The December 1988 issue of *American Historical Review* (93) featured several articles about film and history.

46. To subscribe to H-FILM send a one-line e-mail message to LISTSERV@UICVM.UIC.EDU with the message SUBSCRIBE H-FILM and your name.

47. Daniel J. Walkowitz, 'Telling the Story: The Media, the Public, and American History," *Perspectives* (American Historical Association newsletter) 31 (October 1993), pp. 1, 6–7; Robert Brent Toplin, "Editor's Report: History and the Media, 1993," *Journal of American History* 80 (December 1993), pp. 1175–1178.

48. "Object-centered inquiries typically utilize material documentary evidence to explain the meaning of the object in and of itself; object-driven studies take the evidence and questions generated by material culture and extend them into a broader inquiry aimed at the interpretation of society and culture." Bernard L. Herman, "The Discourse of Objects," in his *The Stolen House* (Charlottesville: University Press of Virginia, 1992), p. 11.

The MARC Format and Electronic Reference Images: Experiences from the Library of Congress Prints and Photographs Division

by **Marcy Flynn and Helena Zinkham**

INTRODUCTION

Since 1982, the Library of Congress Prints and Photographs Division (P&P) has been recording selected collections in electronic form and cataloging them for reference access.[1] The work began while the MARC format for Visual Materials was still being defined, but even the automated records for the first collections paralleled the MARC format data categories, and these early records are now being converted to the MARC format. Records for electronic image collections cataloged since 1988 are created directly in the MARC format in either the Library's central catalog (MUMS) or in a PC software (Minaret) and then combined in a single retrieval system. The electronic reference images began with videodiscs[2] and are gradually being replaced with digital image files.

In every project there are choices about what data to include in a catalog record, how to make use of preliminary inventories (both handwritten and automated documents), level of cataloging detail, and retrieval system options for indexing and displaying the data. This paper's description of some of P&P's choices and how they are evolving as the MARC format and retrieval systems develop should help to clarify issues in using the MARC format with electronic image reference surrogates to improve access to pictorial materials in libraries. Electronic imaging is a rapidly growing and changing area, and many libraries now have imaging projects.[3] This paper focuses on a variety of cataloging issues.

CATALOGING CONTEXT

P&P's cataloging is done in the context of a large and varied research collection of more than thirteen million unpublished and published photographs, cartoons, posters, ephemera, documentary and architectural drawings, and historical and fine prints. Most of the images are photographs related to the United States, but many foreign countries and many time periods are represented. Some eight hundred people consult the collections in the P&P Reading Room each month, in addition to several hundred others who make inquiries by phone and by mail.

The catalog records must be flexible enough to handle a wide variety of information. They must also balance the reference service need for self-explanatory, self-sufficient captions for each image (with a preference for direct item-level access) and the strong desire to make many more P&P collections available. By necessity there are preliminary as well as full-level cataloging records. Due to decades of understaffing and lack of standards, P&P has "only" five million images accessible so far, most through group cataloging in card or online catalogs, or in self-indexing browsing files of mounted photographs and prints, without item-level description or control. Almost half a million items now have electronic reference images; most of them still need electronic captions.

Many of P&P's holdings are arranged in archival groupings by provenance and are appropriate for group cataloging to describe the common features that make the individual images comprehensible. The large groups are usually accompanied by a paper finding aid with brief entries at the folder or item level. Many other items, received from many sources, have been gathered in filing series by physical format or subject, for example, panoramic photographs or cartoon drawings. Such fragile, high research value material warrants item-level records in order to prevent frequent handling of original images. P&P has now begun to combine group- and item-level records in a single retrieval system to replace a heritage of numerous separate and idiosyncratic card catalogs. The automated records still reflect, however, various depths of description and indexing depending on research value of the material, resources for cataloging, and the amount of available information.

Our choice of the MARC format for cataloging reflects three goals for expanding access to visual collections: (1) to create records that can be integrated readily with the Library of Congress (LC) central catalog of books, maps, movies, sound recordings, and other materials; (2) to create records that can be distributed to the national bibliographic networks and integrated with records for graphic materials and print materials at other institutions; (3) to create records for items in one collection that can be combined readily with records from many other collections, because the MARC data is tagged in a way that is recognized by existing catalog programs and that results in similar display and indexing of data.

No information has been needed that could not be included in a MARC record. However, better solutions to redundant data for similar items within a single collection and solutions to the loss of collection context for individually cataloged items will be necessary so that users can navigate the growing quantity of records in catalogs. The Research Libraries Group's new Digital Image Access Project is actively exploring these issues.[4] With current cataloging systems and with certain kinds of collection processing workflows, however, P&P has thus far found it practical to compile information for each item and bring together images in a related group through common headings in the catalog.[5]

ELECTRONIC IMAGING CHOICES

The provision of electronic images as reference surrogates is the modern equivalent of pasting tiny photographs on catalog cards or using aperture cards. Visual surrogates are by far the most effective means for making original visual collections accessible while protecting them from unnecessary handling. The electronic image format can be videodiscs, CD-ROMs, Photo CDs, or online digital files. For P&P, the ability to link automated catalog records with electronic images, the capacity to store huge numbers of images in a compact electronic format, and the durability of electronic images are among the factors that have outweighed their current relatively low resolution. Videodisc resolution is comparable to a television display; the digital formats offer equivalent or higher resolution.[6]

P&P does not make electronic surrogates for all collections. The reasons include: sheer quantity of items, the need to have textual information and details on images legible, state of the technology, copyright and other restrictions, cost, and inappropriateness of electronic images for certain materials. A newspaper morgue with a million photographic prints was recently processed by compiling a printed folder-level finding aid with word processing software. In this case, the original photographs are not too fragile for researchers to handle. It took several project staff members two years just to compile the finding aid from the headings on each folder; it would have taken an inordinate number of people and years to have reproduced each image (and the associated information on the back) electronically. In addition, reproduction rights for the wire press service and commercial firm photographs would also need to be checked image by image before the electronic images could be shown beyond P&P's Reading Room. P&P also continues to microfilm some collections when, for example, extensive handwritten or typed captions are present with the images and separate item-level captions would be difficult to incorporate in a finding aid.

Since electronic image technology remains too expensive to apply to all P&P collections at once, it is used chiefly for material that is unsafe or unwieldy to serve in its original form or that warrants a color surrogate (for example, film and glass negatives, daguerreotypes, panoramas, and posters). Collections were chosen for videodisc projects for several reasons: they were otherwise unavailable for public use, they had high research value, and they were difficult to serve in their original fragile formats. For the most part, entire collections rather than selected parts have been reproduced in order to maintain their integrity and to make the material available for primary historical research.

The production steps established in the 1980s are still followed. A contractor films the material on site and then converts each frame of 35mm film to a videodisc frame, and more recently, to a set of digital image files: a small uncompressed thumbnail, a compressed screen-size reference image, and an uncompressed backup image. The resolution ranges from 560 × 420 pixels (oldest projects) to 1024 × 768 pixels (newest projects). As higher resolutions become affordable for image capture, storage, display, and transmission, new collections will be recorded at those higher levels. High resolution digital cameras hold promise for the capability to scan material without a film intermediate.[7] None of the P&P collections selected thus far for electronic copying could have been handled in a flat bed scanner. (Videodisc production steps are described in Appendix A; current LC digital image file specifications are listed in Appendix B.)

P&P PROJECTS

P&P has recorded thirteen collections and created more than 100,000 records for individual photographs, posters, cartoon drawings, and architectural drawings on seven videodiscs. The records and images are available at an online public access catalog, informally called the "One-Box catalog," that has been in the planning stages since 1988 and reached the P&P Reading Room in December 1993. It provides touch-screen access to user friendly displays; browseable indexes for creators, titles, subjects, call numbers, and reproduction numbers; and free text retrieval for all of P&P's automated cataloging and electronic images.

The One-Box catalog combines P&P records from LC's central catalog (MUMS) with records from a PC database software (Minaret); records with and without associated videodisc images; and many types of records: guide records for entire collections, full-level cataloging for groups of related images, minimal level cataloging for single items, and preliminary-level finding aid captions. At the time of this writing (June 1994), the One-Box is in an interim phase available only in P&P's Reading Room at a public workstation that will come to have digital images and run on client-server architecture. It may be expanded to other LC special collections and in the very long term could provide access to LC's entire catalog. The P&P records and images might also be linked to LC's central catalog, at least as an adjunct resource file.

Work is underway on six more collections with 350,000 images, and a method is being sought to link groups of related images to a single catalog record instead of making individual records for each image when little unique information is available for each image. New projects are creating only digital images rather than videodiscs. The images first captured for videodisc are also being converted to digital files in order to make them more accessible by incorporating them in LC's digital library program. Digital images of works without known copyright restrictions are offered on the Internet;[8] other distribution could include national bibliographic networks and CD-ROM publications. The American Memory Project has made several videodiscs available at its pilot library sites. These and other discs that have been finished in the past year seem more likely to be distributed now through digital image systems than through published videodiscs.[9]

Advanced technology has not yet minimized the hours of labor necessary for image capture and cataloging. The cost per frame varies depending on the difficulty of filming. The more uniform the original items are in size and pictorial characteristics, the lower the cost to copy them. Significant costs really lie in physically preparing the material, inventorying, filming quality control, and cataloging. And, although project organizers seem instinctively to worry about the labor and cost of putting images on disks, physical processing and cataloging costs are often the largest expense and consume the most staff time. Without the preparatory physical organization and the cataloging, the electronic images are of little use.

CATALOGING DATA AND FIELDS

In determining how to proceed, P&P cataloging, curatorial, and reference staff develop consensus on which information to record and on wording for "default" data in each bibliographic record. Such default (or boilerplate) information varies with each project but often includes such data as the creator's name, collection name, provenance, physical medium, commercial reproduction restriction notes, and standard fixed field values. After all the data has been compiled, there are usually some global changes to update subject headings or to add or delete a stock note. For example, the MARC format Host-Item linking field (field 773) was globally added to item records to link them to the single general collection record that provides helpful summaries of date spans, overall subject matter, and background information. (Sample item and collection records in Appendixes C and D illustrate this field usage and many of the following field examples.)

Many innovations in cataloging and retrieval systems have occurred since P&P first made records for images on videodisc by capturing data in word processing software and loading it into a PC database software (called BRS) for use in a local online PC catalog. These BRS records were defined with fields that were parallel to MARC format fields but without any leader information, indicators, or subfield coding. Computer space constraints caused such descriptive data as statements of responsibility and subject notes to be omitted. Reliance was placed on the information in main and added entry fields; in form, genre and subject headings; and in videodisc "visual reference images."[10]

These "caption" records are proving relatively straightforward to convert to the MARC format, although they are being coded as preliminary records to reflect the fact that their headings are ten years old and some now conflict with headings used in other cataloging. If the preliminary subject headings vary greatly from the LC *Thesaurus for Graphic Materials* and cannot be efficiently updated, they are coded as Index Term—Uncontrolled (field 653). It should be kept in mind that some systems may index the Uncontrolled Index Term field as a subject and others may index it as a note. If the preliminary subject headings are earlier forms of valid headings (represented in the thesaurus by cross references), the record is coded as preliminary, and the subject heading is left in the Subject Added Entry—Topical Term (field 650). A major question that remains to be resolved is the impact of such preliminary record headings in a catalog where most headings do not conflict with headings in LC's central catalog. Is this situation a valid variation on multiple thesauri used in a single catalog? Should these collection finding aids with older headings be isolated into separate searching files?

When LC implemented the MARC format for Visual Materials in 1986, P&P began to enter into LC's central catalog many full-level cataloging records for groups of photographs, chiefly views by Frances Benjamin Johnston, copyright deposit images of Native Americans, and photographic albums. (All group-level cataloging is full-level description and indexing.) These five hundred records refer to more than two million photographs and are not directly associated with images on optical disks unless a single item has a copy negative that appears on the copy negative videodiscs with an item-level record.

In cataloging images with electronic reference surrogates, P&P continues to follow basic library cataloging standards, with some flexibility for the preliminary level finding aids. The core tools are: *Anglo-American Cataloguing Rules* and its supplement, *Graphic Materials: Rules for Describing Original Items and Historical Collections*; controlled subject headings from *LC Thesaurus for Graphic Materials* and *Descriptive Terms for Graphic Materials*; proper noun name headings from the Library of Congress *Subject Headings* and name authority files; and the *USMARC Format for Bibliographic Data*. On a project-by-project basis, decisions are made about what information is needed in the records. That information shapes the decision about providing full-level or minimal-level cataloging, or preliminary-level finding aid records. Each project has its own "data dictionary" that documents data conventions field by field. (A sample dictionary page is in Appendix E.)

Authority work remains important, although a choice is made about whether to fit the proper name headings into the LC central catalog environment (on a "no-conflict" basis or by making authority records with cross references) or whether to make headings consistent within the collection (as in a finding aid index). Consistency of headings *within* each collection project has been achieved, although some headings conflict *across* collections when collection records are combined in the One-Box catalog. Such conflicts are reconciled as they are found.[11]

Titles (field 245) are taken whenever possible from information on or with the material. In the preliminary level records, the titles are often written in formulaic patterns, based on information on a jacket or in a logbook, rather than transcribed strictly. Little research is done to confirm or enhance the caption information, but conflicting information, such as completely different spellings for the same building name, is often checked and resolved. Few subject notes are written when the image can be seen with the record, but cartoon drawings (for example) still benefit from an explanatory subject note. Topical subject headings and genre/form headings are assigned as usual with careful judgement. Proper name subject headings focus on events and places. Depending on the amount of information available and the research focus of each collection, names of buildings and people may be left in titles and notes without establishing a corresponding subject heading.

Geographic place name access and chronological access remain as important as in any cataloging. The desire for access to each level in the country-state-city place name hierarchy and the desire to store place names once in a single field (instead of as subdivisions after each subject heading) led to experiments with the Hierarchical Place Name field (field 752). The field is appropriate for places associated with a particular attribute of the material being cataloged. The rare book and newspaper communities use this field to index the place where a book was printed or the area served by a newspaper. In such applications, the field is indexed as a note to distinguish it from works "about" the place. With photographs (the bulk of visual materials), the place where the image was made matches the place depicted, and the field seems useful for subject indexing. It is hard, though, for a single catalog to index the same field as both a subject and a note.

To assist with chronological access, the fixed-length field for Type of Date/Publication Status (field 008) is used in all levels of cataloging. For the collections reproduced on optical disk it is the only fixed field that is set record by record, and it is used instead of chronological subdivision of subject headings. The fixed field provides a predictable four-digit expression of the year when the original image was created; in the descriptive area for Date of Publication, Distribution, etc. (field 260 subfield c) this information may be expressed with words, hyphens, or question marks that clarify the information for the reader but hinder its automated retrieval. This use of the 008 field to provide chronological subject access works best with photographs, for most of which the creation date and depiction date are the same. For other materials, for example, a poster made in 1970 about an event in 1920, the 008 field indexes the publication year (1970) and access to the subject year (1920) can be lost unless it is conveyed through a subject term for the event.

The mixture of records with subject headings that have chronological and geographic subdivisions (minimal and full level cataloging) with records that lack such subdivisions (preliminary level finding aid cataloging) is also being evaluated. The current P&P researcher and staff reliance on key word retrieval, even for subject headings, means that a search for "BANKS IN NEW YORK" will find the topical and geographic information in both types of records. As the catalog grows, its users may rely more on the alphabetical browseable headings and be confused that only some "BANKS" have geographic and chronological subdivisions. A possible solution would be a catalog designed to display the unsubdivided headings with the geographic and chronological information present in other fields. Since national network catalogs also combine records from many libraries, only some of which subdivide headings, this issue is a general catalog concern.

Some projects depend on information compiled first for checklists printed locally or for books. Rather than catalog from scratch, P&P has built catalog records from word processing texts that were prepared for publications and then added headings and descriptive information to complete the record. Such recycling of data often includes acceptance of some non-standard descriptive cataloging conventions. For example, rather than moving individual words by hand, the phrase "drawing, ink on wove paper" would be automatically converted to "1 drawing : ink on wove paper" instead of the standard format "1 drawing on wove paper : ink." The focus in converting data is on mapping data to the appropriate fields and on updating access points such as subject headings and creator names rather than on refining descriptive information that is coherently expressed.

Record linkage is a major issue in current cataloging planning efforts. What are the most effective techniques for linking a guide record (or collection-level description) down to all of its subgroup and item-level records as well as upwards from item-level records to a general collection guide record, or to any intermediate levels, e.g., an album or architectural project series? The Host-Item Entry field (field 773) links items upwards to the next level of record by including the record control number of the higher level record. A retrieval system could also include special programming to guide catalog users among collections sorted by physical format, broad subject, custodial division, or collection name. Retrieval systems need automated prompts for navigating among the levels.

Another issue is the need to link images and data. Traditional P&P call numbers are usually variable-length "filing series" codes or filing categories established decades ago, rather than unique control numbers that work well for linking images and records. The Avery Library at Columbia University, for instance, has employed its unique accession numbers for the link in a local field called Component Item Entry (field 789). What form, then, should the image control numbers take? When are they added to the records? Into which MARC field do they go?

The first P&P projects used a local Image Identification field (field 938) with subfields for a videodisc number and frame and for descriptive information about the source material used to produce the videodisc. Example:

938 $a LCPP001A-12345 $c DLC $d (from original). A pattern was established to name each disc by the custodial division for the original collection, so that the disc number in combination with the 53,000 pre-assigned frame numbers on each videodisc would create a unique image number. Computer programs direct the videodisc player to display a specified frame, and the discs are manufactured so that players recognize each standard frame location. American Memory projects also used this field for motion picture images on videodisc and added a subfield to specify the last playback frame.

Since the MARC format defined an Electronic Location and Access address field (856) in 1993, P&P has begun to use that field to record the digital file image address. Example: 856 $3 original $d LCPP001A $f 1A12345. A locator table is being designed to list the set and file names from the record and correlate them to the physical electronic image directories, that might be moved over time from one computer to another. The first batches of digital file names will be based on the corresponding videodisc frame numbers, but future file names could be based on accession numbers, negative numbers, or PIN numbers. Many records will use both fields: the local field 938 will remain for images on local videodiscs and field 856 will be added for digital image addresses that can be distributed beyond P&P.

One record can be associated with several images, and conventions have been developed for when to use multiple image location fields and when to use multiple subfields. For panoramas, details of the image are available as well as the entire image. In those cases, the images are in consecutive file sets, easily described in one field. For posters that have been recorded from color slides as well as from black-and-white negatives, or from the entire original poster as well as a from a slide detail, repeatable fields are used for each electronic image to explain the difference in the source materials.

Each record includes a note about the electronic reference surrogate in the Additional Physical Form Available Note (field 530). The stock wording "Use surrogate on videodisc available in the Library of Congress Prints and Photographs Reading Room" directs researchers to use the surrogate rather than the original material. Originals are still served when, for example, researchers need to see physical characteristics or caption texts not apparent in the videodisc. For collections available as digital image files, the stock note wording is "Use electronic surrogate." The collection guide records have a similar note that also describes when the videodisc or digital images were made and from what source material.

Information related to reproduction restrictions is provided in the Terms Governing Use and Reproduction Note (field 540). Such information has long been recorded for many collections, and information sheets that explain the restrictions are kept at the reference desk. Plans for distributing images as well as records has increased our attention to including a short reminder in each item-level record. For collections with a wide variety of reproduction limitations, the stock note states: "May be restricted: Information on reproduction rights available in LC P&P Restrictions Notebook." Other collections may be more clear cut. The Gottscho-Schleisner architectural photograph records state directly, "Restricted: commercial use requires written permission from Mrs. Doris Schleisner, Jamaica, New York, in her lifetime."[12]

CONCLUSION

Catalog records combined with electronic images appeal greatly to P&P's researchers. While there is a desire for higher resolution images, we are most frequently asked to provide more images and more data. The thirteen collections completed thus far have shown the viability of incorporating MARC format cataloging with both videodisc and CD-ROM images in that the same data can be implemented in a variety of public retrieval systems: P&P's online public access catalog (the One-Box), American Memory's PC and Macintosh CD-ROM programs, a commercial CD-ROM publication, and in LC's World Wide Web application for the Internet.

The cataloging issues are generally independent of electronic image issues, except for the image linking fields and the increased need for notes about reproduction restrictions. The desire to enable access to collections by providing electronic surrogates was, however, what prompted many of the P&P projects that raised the cataloging issues described above. The large number of images in these projects inspired investigations of ways to record information more compactly, for example, by using the hierarchical place name field instead of geographic subdivisions. The results of blending group and item-level with full-, minimal-, and preliminary-level records in a single system will be evaluated in the coming year.

Little cataloging has been simplified or speeded so far by producing electronic images to accompany the records, although this impression may reflect P&P's choice to record high research value material for which individual description is merited. Still, the expectation is that with an electronic image catalog, the catalog user will be able to research images in a more efficient manner. The speculative future includes such possibilities as inexpensive, high resolution image systems that could make it feasible to scan captions as well as images, so that the images in an archival group are sufficiently self-identifying to rely on group-level cataloging. Another possibility is the further development of hierarchically linked cataloging to clarify collection/group-level information and avoid redundant information at the item-level. P&P will continue to participate with other libraries in this exciting development of more effective catalogs for pictorial research collections.

NOTES

1. This work has been supported by several Library of Congress activities: the Optical Disk Pilot Program, the American Memory Program, and the Deteriorating Negatives Project. Along with P&P staff, staff from American Memory, the Automation Liaison and Planning Office, and Information Technology Services have also been active participants in planning and development. In most cases, the processing and cataloging effort has also been a part of the Arrearage Reduction Program.

2. Analog laser videodiscs were selected in 1982 because they were off-the-shelf technology and, as a storage medium, offered the highest capacity at that time.

3. Current project profiles often appear on the Internet, for example, the Clearinghouse of Image Databases (gopher to dizzy.library@arizona.edu). Published descriptions of a few representative projects are cited in the bibliography.

4. This one year collaborative project began in 1993 to explore the capabilities of digital image technology for managing access to photographic collections. Nine research libraries are each contributing 1,000 photographs of the urban landscape. A general record for each collection will be created for the Research Libraries Information Network (RLIN). A separate database is being developed that liinks collection, series, and item records for efficient finding aid data entry and display. Only information that is unique at a particular record level need be entered at that level. The level at which the same type of information is recorded can vary from collection to collection. The item-level record, for example, may contain as little information as the electronic image identification number and as much information as a typical bibliographic record. A CD-ROM of the images and database will allow participants to test the results in their libraries. A symposium with published proceedings is also planned.

5. During the Optical Disk Pilot Program, P&P created some group records with item-level contents notes (field 505). It proved difficult for researchers to associate a displayed image with its corresponding caption located somewhere in a content note, expecially for groups of more than ten items whose long catalog record filled several display screens. Alternative approaches include the Avery Architectural and Fine Arts Library use of a local RLIN field called Component-Item Entry (field 789) to describe architectural drawings that are part of a project set. This technique is more effective than a single long contents note because a separate field describes each item, with subfields to identify specific types of descriptive information such as title, creator, medium, and identification number. Special display or indexing programs could be developed to correlate each image and its description. Another approach proposed by the University of California Berkeley would place finding aids online as Standard Generalized Markup Language (SGML) coded documents: the group level MARC catalog records would link to the corresponding eletronic image. The RLG Digital Image Access Project offers an approach that would allow a subject heading or creator or other image attribute that applies to only a few items in a group to point directly to those items rather than to the entire group.

6. The bibliography cites representative articles on videodisc and digital imaging by Austin, Besser, and Robinson.

7. Direct digital scanning of cartoon drawings and photographic negatives at the National Archives of Canada is described in an article by Gerald Stone, cited in the bibliography.

8. The address for the Library of Congress, World Wide Web, Mosaic home page is: http://cweb.loc.gov/homepage/lchp.html.

9. A description of the American Memory Program is cited in the bibliography. The first CD-ROM

publication is *Selected Civil War Photographs, 1861–1865: A Multimedia CD-ROM. An American Memory Collection from the Library of Congress* (Austin, TX: Stokes Imaging Services, 1994).

10. For a full description of this project, see the article by Elisabeth Betz Parker cited in the bibliography.

11. The availability of a single alphabetically browseable list of headings from the many collections in the One-Box retrieval system has also reminded staff of the large investment required for accurate data. The browsing list is a valuable proofreading tool for such minor typographical errors as omitting a comma between a photographer's name and birth date and such critical errors as reversing numerals in a birth date.

12. Many of these cataloging issues were described in the American Memory context in a paper by Carl Fleischhauer, cited in the bibliography.

APPENDIX A

Videodisc Production Outline and Quality Control Procedures for Evaluating Workprints and Alpha Discs

Library of Congress, Prints & Photographs Division
February 1993

1. INTRODUCTION & PURPOSE

Videodisc production in P&P began with the Optical Disk Pilot Program in 1982. The primary purposes of producing a videodisc are to improve access by creating a reference surrogate of a collection and to aid preservation by reducing handling of original materials. Each collection reproduced on videodisc thus far has had unique characteristics demanding different production procedures. The varying requirements are outlined in each videodisc production contract. This chapter describes only basic procedures common to all of P&P's videodisc projects. An outline of the entire production process is listed below.

2. SUMMARY OF VIDEODISC PRODUCTION

- Selection of a collection (assignment of processing priority)
    - Identify goals for the collection
    - Determine if videodisc is an appropriate reference surrogate
- Survey
    - Determine size, format, quantity, location and condition of the collection
    - Review background information
    - Develop processing plan
- Request for proposal (RFP)
    - Describe intended final product(s)

60 / VISUAL RESOURCES

- - Determine if to be in color or black-and-white, whether masking is required, whether enhancement is required and where make-ups are placed
  - Define sequence, presentation order, disc user codes, targets, and packaging
- Contract
  - Evaluate proposals
  - Select contractor
  - Review work plan supplied by contractor
- Production
  - Prepare materials (label, inventory, conserve)
  - Capture images (contractor)
  - Evaluate test samples (videotape or workprint)
  - Evaluate workprint and/or videotape
  - Reshoot corrections (contractor)
  - Evaluate reshoots
  - Evaluate Alpha disc
- Finale
  - Distribution of disc
  - Publicity
  - Celebration

3. REQUIRED EQUIPMENT & MATERIALS

A videodisc player, video monitor and a finding aid are needed to use a disc. A finding aid is usually in the form of a descriptive record entered into a full-text searchable database. The database includes videodisc frame numbers so that corresponding records and images can be displayed. A finding aid can also be in the form of a disc map provided by the contractor. A disc map is an itemized list of the items in a collection and their corresponding videodisc frame numbers.

4. PHYSICAL PREPARATION PRIOR TO FILMING

Ideally, the collection should be entirely processed prior to filming. The contractor filming and producing the videodisc should know in advance the formats, quantity, and peculiarities of the collection to efficiently produce a disc free of errors. However, if deadlines are a concern, the following steps are required before any item can be filmed.

A. LABELING—Mark each item or its housing with a unique identifying number.

B. INVENTORY—Create a master inventory of the collection. The contractor may use this to create a database, track overall progress and determine filming schedules. The inventory is used as an item level checklist throughout all production stages.

C. CONSERVATION—Ensure that every item is in stable physical condition and can be handled and photographed safely.

5. WORKPRINT EVALUATION

After filming, the contractor supplies a workprint (i.e., a positive 35mm film) to be evaluated. P&P staff are responsible for checking both the overall quality of the print and specific problems related to each original. Workprints are also called check prints.

Evaluation of the workprint requires a *sweep check* and a *spot check*.

The sweep check is a complete evaluation of every image on the workprint. Use a microfilm reader to detect orientation problems, blank frames, and physical defects.

Spot checks are visual one-to-one comparisons between the workprint images and the originals. One image from every fifty or at least one image from each filming session is evaluated. Use a light table and a photographic loupe to identify problems in contrast, density, and color balance. A gray scale (and a color chart when applicable) on the workprint are also evaluated on the light table.

All problems discovered during the sweep check and spot check are recorded on a *problem worksheet*. A comparison between the check print and the original determines if the identified problem is a function of the original or if the problem has occurred during the filming or check print production process.

Problems due to the conditions of the originals are edited out and the remaining list becomes the *correction list*. P&P then submits the correction list to the contractor.

From the correction list the contractor returns a *reshoot list* which identifies only those originals from the correction list which must be refilmed. Other corrections are made through electronic manipulation, e.g. changing the orientation from vertical to horizontal.

After all items are refilmed, the contractor will supply another check print for evaluation. This print is evaluated entirely on the light table with the correction list being used as a guide to determine that all problems have been corrected. Be aware that new or different problems could occur during the reshoot process.

6. ALPHA DISC EVALUATION

The Alpha Disc is a "first-draft" copy of the final disc. The Alpha disc should replicate the exact order and format of the final disc.

The evaluation of the Alpha disc mirrors procedures for evaluation of the check print. Both sweep checks and spot checks are necessary and all problems are once again recorded on a problem worksheet.

Reshoots may still be necessary after Alpha Disc production, and depending on the amount of remaining corrections, the contractor may elect to produce a second Alpha Disc prior to final disc pressing.

APPENDIX B

Specifications for Digital Images
Library of Congress
July 1993

Image formats:

UNCOMPRESSED IMAGES
Screen-size (ranging from 560×420 to 1024×768)
B&W images at 8 bits per pixel (bpp)
Color images at 24 bpp
Uncompressed
TIFF version 5.0 headers

REFERENCE IMAGES
Screen-size (ranging from 560×420 to 1024×768)
B&W images at 8 bpp
Color images at 24 bpp
B&W images at 10:1 compression ("level A")
Color images at 20:1 compression ("level B")
JPEG compression
JFIF headers

THUMBNAIL IMAGES
No dimension greater than 150
Both B&W and color thumbnails at 8 bpp

Color palette optimized (adaptive palettes) for each image
Uncompressed
TIFF version 5.0 headers

FOR ALL IMAGES: The file name extensions are .JPG for compressed images and .TIF for uncompressed images.

Image file headers

TIFF tag	Description	Content	Example
010D	ID	[set and file name]	LCPP006A 6A24678
013B	Creator	Library of Congress	Library of Congress
0132	Date	year scanned	1993

The file name is also included in the JFIF header.

Delivery Medium

Write-once CD-ROM.

APPENDIX C

Sample Item-level Finding Aid Record with MARC Content Designation for Figure 1.

Panoramic Photograph Collection

Leader [05] n [06] k [07] d [17] 5 [18] a
005 19930813133702.0
007 [00] k [01] h [02] | [03] | [04] | [05] |
008 [00] 900726 [06] s [07] 1919 [18] nnn [33] k [34] n [15] | | [22] | [23] | | | | |
[28] | [35] | | |

001	$a pan93001200 $b PP
017	$a J234710 $b U.S. Copyright Office
037	$a LC-USZ62-54447 $b DLC $c (b&w film copy neg. of left section)
037	$a LC-USZ62-54448 $b DLC $c (b&w film copy neg. of right section)
040	$a DLC $c DLC $e gihc
050 00	$a PAN US GEOG - Texas, no. 43 $u (E size) <P&P> USE VIDEODISC

64 / VISUAL RESOURCES

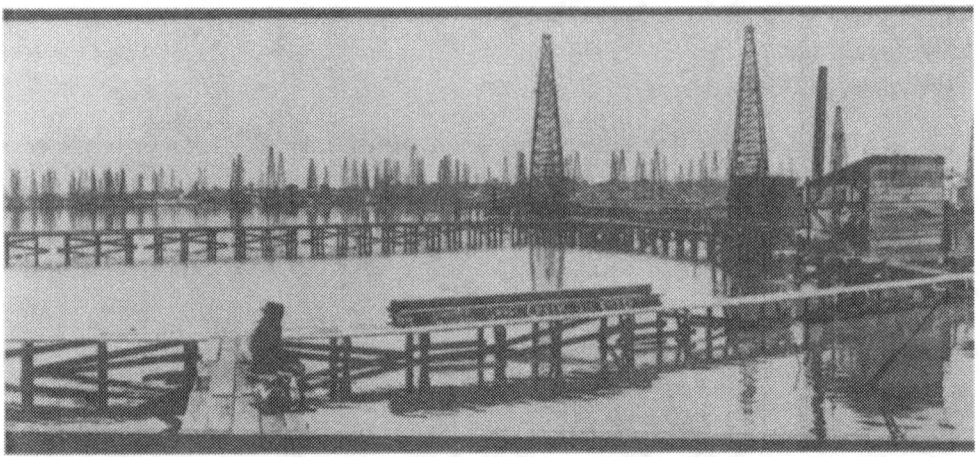

Figure 1. Goose Creek Oil Field, Baytown, Texas. Panoramic photograph, copyrighted by F.J. Schlueter, 1919. Library of Congress, Prints and Photographs Division. (Negative no. LC-USZ62-54447 and LC-USZ62-5448.) (Courtesy of the Library of Congress)

245	00	$a Goose Creek Oil Field $h [graphic].
260		$c c 1919.
300		$a 1 photographic print : $b silver gelatin ; $c 8 × 47 in.
500		$a Copyright claimant's address: Houston, Texas.
530		$a Use surrogate on videodisc available in the Library of Congress Prints and Photographs Reading Room.
540		$a Copyright not renewed (verified 1992/93).
541		$c Copyright deposit ;$a F. J. Schlueter ;$d June 2, 1919.
650	7	$a Oil wells. $2 lctgm
650	7	$a Petroleum industry. $2 lctgm
650	7	$a Piers & wharves. $2 lctgm
700	1	$a Schlueter, F. J. (Frank J.), $e copyright claimant.
752		$a United States $b Texas $d Baytown.
755		$a Panoramic photographs. $2 gmgpc
755		$a Silver gelatin prints. $2 gmgpc
773	0	$t Panoramic photographs (Library of Congress) $w (DLC) 93845487
856		$3 original $d LCPP006A $f 6A10083 $g 6A10092
856		$3 b&w film copy neg. of left section $d LCPP003B $f 3B02394
856		$3 b&w film copy neg. of right section $d LCPP003B $f 3B02395
938		$a LCPP006A-10083 $c 10 images $b DLC P&P $d (from original)

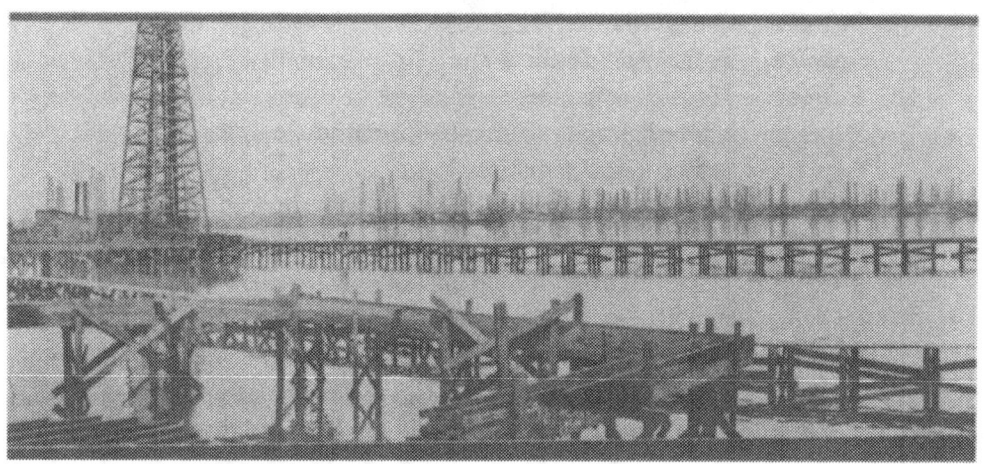

Figure 1. Continued

938    $a LCPP003B-02394 $b DLC P&P $d (from b&w film copy neg. of left section)
938    $a LCPP003B-02395 $b DLC P&P $d (from b&w film copy neg. of right section)
985    $a PP/Pan $e AmMem

Same Record As It Appears in the One-Box Catalog

Your Subject search was: Oil wells   (Item 48 of 95)
            Title: Goose Creek Oil Field
   Call Number: PAN US GEOG - Texas, no. 43 (E size) <P&P> USE VIDEODISC
Reproduction #:   LC-USZ62-54447 (b&w film copy neg. of left section)
                       LC-USZ62-54448 (b&w film copy neg. of right section)
    Restriction: Copyright not renewed (verified 1992/93)
       Medium: 1 photographic print : silver gelatin ; 8 × 47 in.
          Date: c 1919
  Related Name: Schlueter, F. J. (Frank J.), copyright claimant.
           Note: Copyright claimant's address: Houston, Texas.
           Note: Use surrogate on videodisc available in the Library of Congress Prints and Photographs Reading Room.
           Note: Copyright deposit June 2, 1919 F. J. Schlueter.
           Note: J234710 U.S. Copyright Office.

Subject: Oil wells
Subject: Petroleum industry
Subject: Piers & wharves
Subject: United States—Texas—Baytown
Format: Silver gelatin prints
Format: Panoramic photographs
Frame Id: LCPP006A-10083 10 images (from original)
Frame Id: LCPP003B-02394 (from b&w film copy neg. of left section)
Frame Id: LCPP003B-02395 (from b&w film copy neg. of right section)
Card #: pan93001200/PP

APPENDIX D

Collection Record with MARC Content Designation

Panorama Photographs

Leader [05] n [06] k [07] c [17] | [18] a
005 19940527122202.0
007 [00] k [01] h [02] | [03] | [04] | [05] |
007 [00] k [01] f [02] | [03] | [04] | [05] |
008 [00] 940523 [06] i [07] 1851 [11] 1991 [18] nnn [33] k [34] n [15] xxu [22] |
[23] | | | | | [28] | [35] eng

001	$a 93-845487 $b PP
040	$a DLC $c DLC $e gihc
043	$a n-us---
050 00	$a Guide Record $u <P&P>
245 00	$a Panoramic photographs (Library of Congress) $h [graphic].
260	$c 1851–1991, bulk 1880–1930.
300	$a ca. 4,250 photographic prints :$b b&w and some color ;$c various sizes, most 28 in. long or longer.
300	$a ca. 75 photomechanical prints :$b b&w and some color ;$c various sizes, most 28 in. long or longer.
351	$a Most panoramas are arranged by size within a filing series called PAN. Further arrangement by subseries (according to broad subject areas): PAN US GEOG, PAN FOR GEOG, PAN SUBJECT, PAN US MILITARY. Panoramas cataloged before 1990 are in the LOT or PH filing series.

555 8	$a Each panorama is described in an automated finding aid with full caption information and subject indexing. An accompanying videodisc reproduces each entire panorama as well as closeups of each section, and includes an introductory video exhibit about making panoramas.
520 0	$a Most are panoramic scenes of the United States and over 20 foreign countries, especially views of towns, cities, and tourist locations, with emphasis on California, New York, Texas, and Illinois. Highlights natural wonders; engineering feats (especially the Panama Canal); and the aftermath of such disasters as fires, earthquakes, and accidents. Includes activities revolving around agriculture, mines, lumber, oil, and other industries. Contains group portraits of school groups, bathing beauties, sports teams, firemen, company picnics, religious groups, professional organizations, convention attendees, and others. Depicts military facilities and related images, taken between and during the first and second world wars. Sporting events, fairs and expositions (the Panama-Pacific International Exposition in particular) are also covered.
500	$a Collection title devised.
500	$a F. J. Bandholtz, Haines Photo Co., Geo. R. Lawrence Co., West Coast Art Co., and Pillsbury Picture Co. are the most prominent photographers/copyright claimants represented in the panoramic photographs.
500	$a All photographs by the Geo. R. Lawrence Co. (including banquet photographs less than 28 inches long) that are known to be in the holdings of the Prints and Photographs Division have been included in this collection since Lawrence's work is closely associated with panoramic photography.
500	$a Specific media forms represented include silver gelatin prints, platinum prints, albumen prints, cyanotypes, collotypes, and halftone photomechanical prints.
500	$a Dimension measurements for image areas of individual panoramas are rounded off to the nearest half inch. Most panoramas are 28 inches long or longer.
500	$a Most panoramas were acquired through copyright deposit. When known, copyright number and information on copyright renewal is provided in item records.
530	$a Use electronic surrogate. Each panorama was copied in sections with 35mm color film and electronically concatenated into a

whole image for a videodisc produced by the Library of Congress, American Memory Program in 1993. The disc is also available in the LC Prints and Photographs Reading Room.

541	$a Copyright deposit and other sources.
650 −7	$a Agriculture $y 1850–2000. $2lctgm
650 −7	$a Civil engineering $y 1850–2000. $2lctgm
650 −7	$a Disasters $y 1850–2000. $2lctgm
650 −7	$a Exhibitions $y 1850–2000. $2lctgm
650 −7	$a Fairs $y 1850–2000. $2lctgm
650 −7	$a Industry $y 1850–2000. $2lctgm
650 −7	$a Meetings $y 1850–2000. $2lctgm
650 −7	$a Military facilities $y 1850–2000. $2lctgm
650 −7	$a Mining $y 1850–2000. $2lctgm
650 −7	$a Sports $y 1850–2000. $2lctgm
650 −7	$a Streets $y 1850–2000. $2lctgm
655 −7	$a Group portraits $y 1850–2000. $2gmgpc
655 −7	$a Landscape photographs $y 1850–2000. $2gmgpc
655 −7	$a Portrait photographs $y 1850–2000. $2gmgpc
700 11	$a Bandholtz, F. J. $q (Frederick J.), $d b. 1877, $e copyright claimant.
710 21	$a Haines Photo Co. (Conneaut, Ohio), $e photographer, $e copyright claimant.
710 21	$a Geo. R. Lawrence Co., $e photographer, $e copyright claimant.
710 21	$a Pillsbury Picture Co., $e copyright claimant.
710 21	$a West Coast Art Co., $e photographer, $e copyright claimant.
755	$a Albumen prints $y 1860–1910. $2gmgpc
755	$a Collodion printing-out paper prints $y 1890–1910. $2gmgpc
755	$a Collotypes $y 1890–1960. $2gmgpc
755	$a Combination prints $y 1900–1940. $2gmgpc
755	$a Cyanotypes $y 1880–1910. $2gmgpc
755	$a Dye coupler prints $y 1990–2000. $2gmgpc
755	$a Gum bichromate prints $y 1890–1910. $2gmgpc
755	$a Halftone photomechanical prints $y 1890–1930. $2gmgpc
755	$a Photomechanical prints $y 1910–1920. $2gmgpc
755	$a Photolithographs $y 1930–1940. $2gmgpc
755	$a Photogravures $y 1910–1920. $2gmgpc
755	$a Photographic prints $y 1850–2000. $2gmgpc
755	$a Platinum prints $y 1890–1920. $2gmgpc
755	$a Silver gelatin prints $y 1850–2000. $2gmgpc
755	$a Silver printing-out paper prints $y 1870–1920. $2gmgpc

755 −7 $a Panoramic photographs $y 1850–2000. $2gmgpc
985      $a PP/Pan $e AmMem

APPENDIX E

Library of Congress, Prints and Photographs Division
Deteriorating Negatives Project
Data Dictionary
Gottscho-Schleisner Collection   3/30/92
MARC Visual Materials Format (MINARET)   rev. 8/03/93

MARC TAG	MARC FIELD NAME
773	Host Item Entry
773/$t	Title
773/$w	Record control Number
773/____1	First indicator-note
773/____2	Second indicator undefined

DEFAULT SCREEN VALUE(S):

Gottscho-Schleisner Collection (Library of Congress) used in $t.
(DLC) 9345488 used in $w.

DATA CONVENTIONS/COMMENTS:

The collection title, **Gottscho-Schleisner Collection (Library of Congress)**, is always in $t. The MUMS control number or LCCN number of the collection-level record is in $w.

The first indicator is **0**, so that this field will display in the record. The second indicator is undefined and is blank.

This field is not implemented currently in MUMS.

PUNCTUATION: none

MINARET AUTHORITY CONTROL: no

EXAMPLE:

773 0 $tGottscho-Schleisner Collection (Library of Congress) $w(DLC) 93845488

BIBLIOGRAPHY

"The American Memory Project: Sharing Unique Collections Electronically," *LC Information Bulletin* (Feb. 26, 1990), pp. 83–87.

Anglo-American Cataloguing Rules, 2nd ed., 1988 rev. (Chicago: American Library Association, 1988–).

Austin, David L., "Videodiscs, Software Indexes, and Reference Services," *Art Reference Services Quarterly*, 1 (1993), pp. 17–25.

Berkeley Finding Aid Project, "Completing the Chain: Linking Finding Aids, Catalogs, & Source Material," Society of American Archivists, Description Section Newsletter *Descriptive Notes*, (Winter 1993–1994), p. 6.

Besser, Howard, "Imaging: Fine Arts," *Journal of the American Society for Information Science*, 42 (Sept. 1991), pp. 589–596.

Evans, Linda J., and Maureen O. Will, comp., *MARC for Archival Visual Materials: A Compendium of Practice* (Chicago: Chicago Historical Society, 1988).

Fleischhauer, Carl, "Bibliographic Records in a Full-content Access System: Some Observations from American Memory's Experience," (June 1993), 35 pp. (Draft paper available through Internet, address: marvel.loc.gov.)

Giral, Angela, "At the Confluence of Three Traditions: Architectural Drawings at the Avery Library," *Library Trends*, 37 (Fall 1988), pp. 232–242.

Lees, Diane, ed., *Museums and Interactive Multimedia: Proceedings of an International Conference Held in Cambridge, England, 20–24 September 1993* (Cambridge: Museum Documentation Association, 1993) (Archives & Museum Informatics Technical Report No. 20)

Library of Congress, Network Development and MARC Standards Office, *USMARC Format for Bibliographic Data* (Washington, D.C.: Library of Congress Cataloging Distribution Service, 1988–).

Newman, Alan B., Deirdre C. Stam, and Christine L. Sundt, eds., "Electronic Visual Imaging in the Museum," *Visual Resources* 7/4 (1991), pp. 291–422. Special issue.

Orbach, Barbara, "So That Others May See: Tools for Cataloging Still Images," *Cataloging & Classification Quarterly*, 11, no. 3/4 (1990), pp. 163–191.

Parker, Elisabeth Betz, comp., *Graphic Materials: Rules for Describing Original Items and Historical Collections* (Washington, D.C.: Library of Congress Cataloging Distribution Service, 1982).

Parker, Elisabeth Betz, comp., *LC Thesaurus for Graphic Materials: Topical Terms for Subject Access* (Washington, D.C.: Library of Congress Cataloging Distribution Service, 1987).

Parker, Elisabeth Betz, "The Library of Congress Non-Print Optical Disk Pilot Program," *Information Technology and Libraries*, 4 (Dec. 1985), pp. 289–299.

Robinson, Peter, *The Digitization of Primary Textual Sources* (Oxford: Office for Humanities Communication, Oxford University Computing Services, 1993).

Shatford, Sara, "Analyzing the Subject of a Picture: A Theoretical Approach," *Cataloging & Classification Quarterly*, 6 (Spring 1986), pp. 39–62.

Snow, Maryly, "Visual Depictions and the Use of MARC." In *Beyond the Book: Extending MARC for Subject Access* (Boston: G.K. Hall, 1990), pp. 225–235.

Stone, Gerald, and Philip Sylvain, "ArchiVISTA: A New Horizon in Providing Access to Visual Records of the National Archives of Canada," *Archivaria*, 33 (Winter 1991–1992), pp. 253–266.

Zinkham, Helena, and Elisabeth Betz Parker, comp., *Descriptive Terms for Graphic Materials: Genre and Physical Characteristic Headings* (Washington, D.C.: Library of Congress Cataloging Distribution Service, 1986).

Information Technology and Access to Visual Images in Printed Books

by Michael Joseph

In his preface to *The National Coordinated Cataloging Program*, Warren J. Haas observed that "cataloging is what turns an accumulation of material into a library collection."[1] Beginnings of modern cataloging practices, which, therefore, form the tap-root of advanced scholarly research, may be traced back to the advent of computer-generated data bases and MARC, an acronym for Machine Readable Cataloging, a cipher for the set of standards for identifying, storing, and communicating cataloging information. The major national computer-generated data bases are, of course, OCLC, the Online Computer Library Center, which became nationally operational in 1971, and RLIN, the Research Libraries Information Network, which followed OCLC into national use at the end of the decade.[2]

RLIN, although the smaller of the two, possesses immeasurably greater flexibility. By allowing a user to scrutinize multiple records describing the same bibliographical item, MARC RLIN facilitates extremely particular communication among catalogers, and represents perhaps the most expressive tool our civilization has ever produced for documenting the evolution and manufacture of publishing history. One RLIN cluster—a concentration of independently generated catalog entries for a single bibliographic item—approximates to a learned stalagtite: perfected over long years by a steady accretion of information.

In 1977, for example, Brown University recorded a piece of American juvenile literature entitled *In the Forest*, published by "L. Prang and Co., Boston" in 1865, describing the book as "a poem for children" and measuring it at "11 by 73 centimeters, folding to 11 by 7 centimeters." According to Brown, whose description is also recorded in NUC, and to the Winterthur Museum, *In the Forest* contained colored illustrations. The Winterthur broadened access to the identity of the publisher, changing L. Prang & Co., to "Prang, Louis & Co. (Boston, Mass.)."

Twelve years later, in 1989, the possibilities of the RLIN database were no longer unexplored and, when the American Antiquarian Society cataloged *In the Forest*, it enriched the online account of the work with several diaphanous layers of complex description. The Society noted that the "colored illustrations" (as previously described) were "chromolithographed,"—a fairly early example of the process in American children's books—as was the text, by Louis Prang (whose birth and death dates are also supplied). The Society's record diligently witnesses "One leaf folded accordion-style to make twelve pages. [and] Leaf consists of two sections pasted together; one folded into eight segments; the other folded into four segments."

The record further notes that Prang issued *In the Forest* in a series denominated the Christmas Stocking Library, with four other titles (bearing copyright dates of either 1864 or 1865), in an 8 × 12 × 6 centimeter stiff-paper box. The Antiquarian Society has integrated into its catalog record the formal elements traditionally associated with descriptive bibliographies and museum exhibition catalogs. The cover of the container for the Christmas Stocking Library is both artful and artfully described, bearing a "series title and design of a Christmas stocking and holly chromolithographed in red, green, and gold ink on a silver background, bordered by a blue frame with gold stars." The volume in hand has itself been poured into a "glazed paper printed wrapper ... printed in purple ink."

Even stout proponents of minimalistic cataloging would agree the Antiquarian Society cataloging record has organized lucid description and analysis with pertinent historical data not readily available elsewhere and placed it within easy reach of interested populations of scholars and researchers. They will jeer at the argument that descriptive cataloging is an interpretive, or hermeneutic act, I daresay, and, I hope, will recoil from the evidence that cataloging may be a form of sacred architecture.

But, before considering shared vocabularies, for a moment let us ponder the visual layout and implications of the catalog record, which, in a certain light, appears to imitate the ideal design of a Gothic cathedral. The focus of the space is similarly compulsive and unrelievedly concentrated. It falls, and falls exclusively upon the "author main entry," much as if, completed by its graven dates of birth and of death, this form of a name were the sign for the priest before the altar-table re-enacting the sacrifice.

Above, the fixed fields radiate from it like the groins of the apse and, concomitantly, just as the ribshafts which receive them and descend to the floor return the eye to the altar table, so, too does the a sudden empty space—created as the vertical column of "variable field" information rises to meet the horizontal or cross-bar of "fixed field" information—sends the eye inevitably back to the "main-entry." Moreover, preceding expressions of vastly divergent information, the main entry is the single line of the record in which definitiveness is certified, much as the priest at the altar-table is illumined by the jeweled-glow of the lancets in the apse.

Below it, for any part of the record, there is always a modicum of uncertainty, much as, wherever the eye may stray in a Gothic cathedral, the Gothic space presents areas of an indefinite beyond, remaining to be explored or abandoned. The main entry is the common center of a cataloging record in which all movement comes voluntarily to rest.

Modern collaborative cataloging is made possible by the inculcation and dissemination of shared vocabularies. The *lingua franca* of cataloging flows from the *Anglo-American Cataloging Rules* first consigned to print in 1967. In its revised second edition, published in 1988, *AACR2r* is augmented by numerous "canonical readings" provided by the Library of Congress, which also sanctions language by which to signify the subject matter of formatted materials in its massive publication, *Subject Headings*. First published in 1909, the sixteenth edition of *LCSH*, issued recently, consists of more than 199,000 entries, spread out over four chunky volumes, "created by catalogers and used in cataloging at the Library of Congress."[3] The conceptual whole toward which the list appears to evolve—without ever gaining—is an alphabetical, democratically collected list of everything, or, a list of everything anyone has ever imagined to write about. Not surprisingly, no small amount of effort is expended by the Subject Headings Editorial Team in the care and feeding of *Subject Headings*, regularly adding hot new terms, dispatching cold fossilized ones, and retooling those that promise to have a little life left in them yet.

One recent *Catalog Service Bulletin*, the element through which LC signals its approval of unusued terms and its obituaries of useless ones, featured thirty-seven examples of the new. Subject searches of potential interest to us can now be made for "Erotic videos," "Maps for children," "Television mini-series," and "Victoriana." Demonstrating conclusively that the volatility of the message is on a par with the medium, the *Bulletin* also included thirty-eight pages of retooled headings, which, though generally keyed to the evolved political status of former Soviet territories, include topics related to nonpolitical embodiments of change as well. (It may be noted in passing that the Art Librarians Society of North America republishes "New and Revised LC Subject Headings" of relevance in its periodical *ARLIS/NA Update*, currently under the byline of Timothy Shipe who heads the LC

Humanities Cataloging Section.) Some news of note: "Mickey Mouse (Cartoon character)" has been cancelled, but "Mickey Mouse (Fictitious character)" will replace it. Similarly, "Ada the Ayrshire (Cartoon character)" will be replaced by "Ada the Ayrshire (Fictitious character)."

You will notice in the replacement of "Cartoon" by "Fictitious" a silting off of form or physical manifestation from topicality. Significant developments to the information technology of graphic arts have occurred, over the last decade, as a compensatory thrust by librarians seeking to provide clearer access to materials, and components of materials, whose essential materiality was deemed of importance to scholarship yet fell prey to the neglect of nineteenth-century Anglo-American cataloging ratiocentricity.

In 1979, two years after the creation of RLIN, cataloging-language-development advanced in the direction of generic and formalized physical description, spurred perhaps by the new possibilities of cataloging in the electronic environment. That year, the Independent Research Libraries Association called for "formats for terms indicating the physical characteristics of the material catalogued."[4] Consequently, in 1980, the Library of Congress submitted a proposal to the American Library Association (ALA) committee for Machine-Readable Bibliographic Information (MARBI) at its March meeting to implement the creation of a field for genre headings, and directed a prototype thesaurus to the Standards Committee (now the Bibliographic Standards Committee) of the Rare Books and Manuscripts Section of the American Council of Research Libraries (ACRL), thereby setting its agenda for the next three years. In June, The American National Standards Institute (ANSI) formulated the guidelines for such thesauri.[5] In 1983 the duly inspired Standards Committee[6] published *Genre Terms: A Thesaurus for Use in Rare Book and Special Collections Cataloging*. *Genre Terms: A Thesaurus* opened avenues of direct access for researchers needing examples of, say, nineteenth-century poems or, even more precise, odes, rather than, say, contemplations of nightingales or unravished brides. *Genre Terms* included visual genres figuring in the history of books, such as "Illustrated works," "Caricatures," "Cartoons," "Catchpenny prints," "Coloring books," "Drawing books," "Livres d'artistes," "Picture novels," "Posters," and "Viewbooks." Thus, in principle, if, having looked at copies of Lynd Ward's *Vertigo*, or *Gods' Man* [sic], researchers wanted to compare it with other examples of this type of work not by Lynd Ward, they could search their local catalog for "Picture Novels." Before, they would have had no recourse from the laborious task of first searching a library's catalog for articles and monographs about Lynd Ward, looking for the names of comparable technicians, or combing in-house example files, and then examining each catalog record or each volume to determine whether they had found a novel in pictures.

Extending the initiative underlying the creation of a MARC field for genre headings (LC-216), in 1983,[7] representatives of MARBI met to review another proposal[8] calling for the implementation of a format tentatively dubbed the Visual Arts Format (I mention this to highlight its visual orientation) but ultimately broadened in scope and christened the Physical Characteristics Access format. Closely allied to Genre headings[9], MARC bibliographic field 755 accepted expressions of precoordinate terms that described physical characteristics of a bibliographic work. The once again inspired Bibliographic Standards Committee passed seven fertile years compiling five additional thesauri whose panorama of terms now assists researchers in locating facets of the decorative arts associated with book manufacture, particularly the antique handicrafts associated with its earlier, developmental periods—commonly called the book arts.

Around the mid-decade mark, Helena Zinkham and Elisabeth Betz Parker responded to the Independent Research Library Association's call to remedy the "lack of vocabulary to index book illustrations"[10] by constructing *Descriptive Terms for Graphic Materials: Genre and Physical Characteristic Headings* (Washington, D.C.: Library of Congress, 1986), which they define as a "single list of standard terms from which catalogers and researchers choose indexing and retrieval vocabulary"[11] In creating **GMGPC**, Zinkham and Parker, who worked together in the Library of Congress Prints and Photographs Division, preferred not to make any attempt at a "theoretical list," but sought "a practical representation of categories of material encountered at the Library of Congress and other extensive American historical collections."[12] The sources of *GMGPC*'s vocabulary included LCSH, as well as the 1984 draft of the *Art and Architecture Thesaurus for Document Types, Drawings and Visual Genre*, the preliminary lists of the Architectural Drawings Advisory Group, and the "personal knowledge of colleagues."[13]

GMGPC consisted of over 500 terms listed alphabetically, in the manner adopted by previous library thesauri, but comprising ten distinct named intellectual categories. In this manifest tendency toward a modular structure— the kind of thesaurus being studied by the Art and Architecture Project— the *GMGPC* demonstrates a movement away from the collectivist, or what we might call, given the nature of the occasion, the "Romanesque" thesaurus, as exemplified by LCSH and the issues of the RBMS Bibliographic Standards Committee; a tendency this paper will presently echo.

Of immediate moment, briefly surveying the ten *GMGPC* categories will suggest their utility as "sight lines" into collections of graphic materials. "Shape and Size" terms look at objects bearing impressive physical features or non-traditional formats, and include "Banners," "Scrolls," and "Video disks." "Status of Production" terms look at the "stage of a process, degree of completion, quantity issued, relationship to other works, and frequency of issue,"[14] and include "Censored works," "Forgeries," and "Studies." "Support Material" terms, the most diminutive and subjective of categories, "indicat[e] primary supports unusual for a physical process," including "Ceramic photographs," "Tintypes," and "Cloth prints."

"Process and Technique" constitutes the most graphic and multifaceted category, including general terms, such as "Collages," "Prints," and "Photographs," and, restrictive terms, such as "Wood engraving," and "Tissue stereographs."

"Purpose," much as the preceding "Process and Technique," is a self-explanatory category looking at a rich variety of materials including "Albums," "Decorations," "Electrical systems drawings," "Fortune Telling Cards," "Games," "Dance Cards," "Plats," "Stats," "Toys," and "Erotica."

The remaining hierarchical categories are "Color aspect," "Component," "Creator"—a small though sovereign group containing just three terms (e.g."Amateur Works") and "Instrument" (e.g. "Detective camera photographs"). The last category, "Method of representation," is internally defined as "expressing a vantage point, degree of finish or formality, or projection type,"[15] and looks at "Aerial photographs," "Allegorical painting," "Cries," "Humorous pictures," "Rebuses," and "Silhouettes."

"Photographs" and "Prints," with which Zinkham and Parker ought to have been most conversant, are, indeed, the most encyclopedic subcategories. Lifting them out from beneath their rubric, "Process and Technique," *GMGPC* usefully provides an index of approximately one hundred terms for specific photographic processes—here again anticipating the structure of the *Art and Architecture Thesaurus*—looking at "Abstract photographs," "Boudoir card photographs," "Motion picture stills," "Still life photographs," "Silver gelatin printing-out paper photoprints," and "Radiographs;" a list of approximately fifty terms for specific "Print" processes matches this, looking at "Drypoints," "A la poupee prints," "Pouchoir prints," "Proofs before letters," "Restrikes," and "Chromolithographs."

With the publication of *GMGPC*, therefore, it became possible for institutions like the American Antiquarian Society to speed examples of the chromolithographs of entrepreneurs like Louis Prang, (publisher/lithographer of *In the Forest*) into the hands of scholars studying topics like America's first attempts at mass-produced color printing processes.

Having grown up in the Prints and Photographs Division of the Library of Congress, beside the *GMGPC*, the *LC Thesaurus for Graphic Materials: Topical Terms for Subject Access*, emerged a year later, a mammoth compilation of 3,567 authorized, or postable terms. The work of Elisabeth Betz

Parker, the LCTGM revised and expanded the author's *Subject Headings Used in the Library of Congress Prints and Photographs Division* (originally issued in 1980). As the *GMGPC* focusses upon varieties of genre, and physical characteristics (G and PC), the *LCTGM*, as Parker defines it, serves "as a tool for indexing and retrieving the subjects of graphic materials" for catalogers and researchers alike.[16] Quite usefully, the latter work absorbed the terms of the earlier.

Among the other sources the *LCTGM* tapped, the then-recently drafted early version of the *Art and Architecture Thesaurus*[17] contributed terms for "indexing pictures of the built environment,"[18] one of the *AAT*'s premier studies. As part of Parker's rationale for constructing the *LCTGM* she cited the insufficiency of terms in *AAT* for a "range of people, events, and activities," which she said "are equally important aspects of general picture collections."[19]

When The Getty Art History Information Program published a three volume set of the *Art & Architecture Thesaurus*, in 1990, correcting the deficiency Parker noted earlier, the *LCTGM* was superseded.[20] The *AAT*, in remarkable contrast to all earlier library thesauri, was envisioned to be a "conceptual whole," consisting of nothing less grand and ambitious than "a set of terms that would include the history and the making of the visual arts."[21] As defined by Toni Petersen, who played a giant role in shaping the *AAT*, both as a co-director from 1980 to 1986, and, since then, as director, its purpose was threefold: To provide

1. Physical description of museum objects, slides, photographs, archival materials, books, drawings.
2. Subject cataloging and keyword indexing of books, images of architecture, images of art, periodical literature.
3. Database searching by scholars, researchers, students, practitioners, librarians, and other information intermediaries.[22]

The vocabulary of the *AAT* derived mainly from four sources, although, when deemed appropriate, in altered form. These include the *Avery Index to Architectural Periodicals, Library of Congress Subject Headings, RIBA Architectural Periodicals Index* and *RILA (International Repertory of the Literature of Art)*.

Structurally akin to the *GMGPC*, the *AAT* resides within a modular organization of seven independent thesauri—defined here, in accord with indexing terminology, as "facets."[23] A facet is "a homogeneous category of terms whose members share characteristics that distinguish them from the members of another facet"[24] and each facet is ascribable within the MARC record to two or more of six usable bibliographic fields, corresponding to access with regard to subject, genre, occupation, function, and physical characteristics. Vocabulary in the *AAT* is adaptive: "Terms from some hierarchies are more appropriate to a given MARC field than others, but since any term could theoretically occur in any field, MARC tags are not pre-assigned to *AAT* terms"[25] as they are in the book-arts and previous graphic arts thesauri.

The seven *AAT* facets bear little resemblance to the ten categories that infrastructure the *GMGPC*, perhaps as a reflection of their dissimilar levels of complexity, purposes, and periods of gestation—the *AAT* boasts of having been conceived in 1979, a long and busy developmental decade before reaching maturity in 1990.

Perhaps the most diverse of orders, "Associated Concepts" provides a lexicon "for abstract concepts, qualities, and phenomena that relate directly to the study and execution of art and architecture [such as "beauty," "balance," and "connoisseurship"], as well as those aligned with other disciplines not directly included in the scope of the thesaurus but useful in relation to art or architecture, such as "metaphor" and "electricity."[26]

"Physical Attributes," a facet embracing *GMGPC*'s categories of "Color Aspect" and "Shape and Size," contains "terms descriptive of the appearance or qualities of artifacts, especially relating to their design or decoration ..."[27]

Browsing the "Color Aspect" hierarchy, or subfacet (containing 296 color descriptors)[28], can be oddly medicating. What one may be in the habit of describing as "reddish orange," the *AAT* describes more perspicaciously as either "vivid reddish orange," or "strong reddish orange," or "deep reddish orange," or "moderate reddish orange," or "dark reddish orange," or "grayish reddish orange." All of these are collectively distinguished from "brownish orange." And the six hues mentioned above comprise what the *AAT* calls the "intermediate orange," and are set apart from the six hues comprising the category "orange."

"Styles and Periods," perhaps the least finished of the facets,[29] contains a broad range of terms for "concepts denoting visually distinctive traits assigned by scholars in the description and classification of man-made works of architecture, fine arts, or decorative arts"[30] including those adopted "from the names of peoples or cultures, geographic areas and sites and the names of rulers and historical periods, as well as terms that are descriptive or interpretive, such as "Black-figure," "Chicago Imagist," "Fantastic Realist" and "Funk."[31]

"Agents," a greatly filled out analogue to the *GMGPC*'s category "Creator," contains terms descriptive of persons or groups ... associated by some role or occupation ["soldier," "sailor," "tinker," "printmaker"] and generic names of groups and organizations."[32] Activities, closely related, contains "terms for actions ... as well as methods ... used to accomplish some end, [including] terms for branches of learning and professional endeavor (archaeology, engineering), conceptually executed processes (analyzing), discrete occurrences and events (contests, death) and processes performed on or with materials and objects (conservation, drawing, weaving). Subsumed within the "Activities" facet is the hierarchy, "Processes and Techniques," somewhat misleadingly bearing a similar name to the major category in *GMGPC*, "Process and technique". But, we do not find "photographs" and "prints" and subcategories thereof listed as genres of illustration processes here. Instead, "photography" and kinds of photography (close-up photography, telephotography, aerial photography) and various print-making techniques are given in nominal form as terms for use in subject access.

Leaping the sixth facet to draw a comparison, one find names for specific kinds of photographs and prints tucked within the sub-subfacet Visual Works of the subfacet Visual and Verbal Communications of the Objects facet, the final facet, which contains descriptors for "inanimate entities that are perceptible ... usually the product of human activity" and "usually associated with aesthetic or symbolic principles."[33]

"Terms for built works and elements of the natural environment ... ("arches," "rivers"), man-made artifacts, including those with a utilitarian purpose, such as tools"[34] are also located within the "Objects" facet. Various terms from *GMGPC*'s "Instrument," "Purpose," and "Method of Representation" categories are brought together here as well. Among the vast array of riches in the *AAT*, terms concentrated within the "Objects" facet are traditionally the most prepossessing for researchers working in the field of graphic and fine arts.

Leaping back, the penultimate facet, "Materials," contains "terms for naturally or synthetically derived substances ... [ranging] from names of raw materials ("iron," "clay") and functional classes of materials ("adhesives," "emulsifiers") to manufactured materials and products ("artificial ivory," "millwork") used in the construction of various objects and components."[35]

Looking at the seven facets arrayed together, from "Associated Concepts" to "Objects," the citation order would seem to mirror the creative act, itself, from conception to objectification; a logical metonymn for the *AAT*'s conceptual wholeness.

Perhaps one of the innovations the *AAT* brings to descriptive cataloging is its faceted structure, whereby terms from different facets may be strung together to achieve precise description and expedite research. As illustrated in the *Thesaurus*'s introductory comparison:

> LCSH terms are pre-coordinated: they are complex concepts put together at the time the heading is generated, and they remain in the authority list in that specific combination. e.g. Wooden doors is an *LCSH* heading, as is Renaissance Painting. In the *AAT* because of its faceted structure, wood is found in the "Materials hierarchy," doors in the "Built works Components hierarchy," Renaissance in the "Styles and Periods hierarchy," and painting in the "Disciplines hierarchy,"[36]

Therefore, by design, a cataloguer/researcher could build/search for the *LSCH* expression, "Renaissance Painting," as well as the non-*LSCH* expression, "Renaissance Wood engraving" or, by adding a term from the "Styles and periods hierarachy," "Italian Renaissance Wood-engraving." The *AAT*'s "'atomized' indexing vocabulary" (MARBI 88-10 3), permits the construction of "bespoke" complex expressions according to the needs of the collection and the intricacy of the indexing system at hand.

If I saw a need to modify the Antiquarian Society record of *In the Forest*, in order to make it more useful for researchers in paper history, I could construct "glazed book paper" by joining "glazed" from the "Processes and Techniques" hierarchy and "book paper" from the "Materials facet." By adding "North American" from the Periods and Styles facet, I would arrive at the heading "North American glazed book paper." The *AAT* also allows me to note that the wrappers have been put through the printing process in the fully synthesized heading: "Printed North American glazed book paper." Although it has already been deemed justifiable to note that the "glazed paper printed wrapper" had been "printed in purple ink," it might not behoove me to create an additional access point for "Purple printing ink." But, I could! (Unless I preferred "Tyrian purple" or "Dark reddish purple"). Furthermore, if I cataloged *In the Forest* on a national utility, each of the terms, in each string, (e.g. "Printed" "North American," "glazed" and "book paper"), would be tagged individually allowing for maximal retrieval, a feature hinging upon the greater capacity of micro-computers.[37]

Clearly, the extent to which the *AAT* can be manipulated by a reasonably knowledgeable technician allows for a measure of precision and detail unattainable with previous access aids. Moreover, despite its complexity, the *AAT* offers ease of use. By dint of its constitutive structure, in which the many elements combine to form a single unified entity, the *AAT* offers information providers a more comprehensible descriptive tool, allowing them to zero in on the desired concept or characteristic. (e.g., while the *AAT* can precede Synthetic Cubism with Analytic Cubism, a dictionary catalog can only follow Synthetic Cubism with the unhelpful term, Synthetic Detergent.)

Therefore, considering the significant advantages to research inherent in using the *AAT*, it is surprising to find it generally neglected. Few institutions have adopted the *AAT* on even a marginal basis. A User Survey planned and sponsored by the *AAT* Advisory Committee of ARLIS/NA and the *AAT*, inaugurated in the fall of 1992, "mailed questionnaires to 4,500 archives, libraries, museums, visual resources collections, indexing services, bibliographic utilities, encyclopedias, dictionaries and inventories."[38] A mere eight percent of these responded to the survey, a total of just over 400, chiefly comprising libraries, visual resources collections, archives, and museums. Just over half of the respondents (56.3%) (or just over 200 institutions) even owned the *AAT* printed edition (1990) and only 39% (or about 312 libraries) said they were using it.[39]

There are many explanations for the *AAT*'s general neglect.[40] Its elaborate architecture and dense and finicky vocabulary combine to give the *AAT* an unfamiliar aspect rather more like the mystical *Cabala* than many libraries might prefer and may be partly responsible for discouraging some. And many libraries have developed their own lists or invested in other vocabularies to which they are committed. Cataloging procedures, like religious art, tend to reproduce themselves, and change comes to them only in the fullness of time. But, inasmuch as the more conventional form and genre thesauri of the eighties have themselves been received with only modest warmth by American research libraries,—in fact, only four examples of "Picture novels" have been labeled in RLIN—obviously other issues are involved.

One, of course, has been the reluctance of library administrators to favor producing cataloging records at the level of complexity attained during the previous decade. Some of the justifications that are routinely advanced for the evacuation of descriptive cataloging savor of a kind of wishful thinking; yet, full-cataloging entails high costs and, during times of library entrenchment, it must undergo critical reevaluation beside every other library service. As has been pointed out, within the University, "libraries consume large quantities of the monetary resources ... and compete with other valuable activities for limited funds."[41]

As long as the library continues to command a declining share of general expenditures within the university budget, librarians must make hard choices about which services we will continue to be able to provide. As the RLG Mid-Decade Planning Group ominously declared, in its First Report, issued in May of 1993: "The system as we know it is becoming less and less affordable."[42]

In the area of professional training, a factor of no mean importance to the long range goals of assembling the visual images of the human record, there is an even greater challenge arising. In the 1980s, post-graduate training for hands-on librarians grew significantly. In the summer of 1983, Terry Belanger, then of Columbia University, launched RBS, Rare Book School. His curriculum included a course entitled "Book Illustration to the Year 1880," which featured "The identification of illustration processes and techniques, including wood-cut, etching, engraving, stipple, aquatint, mezzotint, lithoggaphy, color printing, process relief prints, and photogravure."[43]

As we approach the mid 1990s, as valuable as RBS continues to be to us at the University of Virginia, the catalyst for its migration, the crashing of Columbia University's Library School, continues to give us pause. Professional librarians and information specialists do indeed organize advanced training in seminars and programs supported by a range of institutions and professional organizations, such as the Lilly Library, the American Antiquarian Society, Society of American Archivists, ARLIS, PACSCL, The Rare Book and Manuscript Section of the ACRL/ALA, to quickly point out just a few. But, the increasing failure of major American universities to continue programs of library instruction at the graduate level will erode the informational superstructure at its foundation and strike at the future of advanced research. Scholars in the visual arts must be concerned. As librarianship is threatened with the same cultural marginalization that befell other once beloved, university nurtured disciplines, such as surveying, mining, and ethics, control over our expanding collections verges on de-evolving into, what Warren J. Hass has termed, "an accumulation of material."

SELECTED BIBLIOGRAPHY OF WORKS CITED

Art and Architecture Thesaurus. (New York: Oxford University Press, 1990).

Art Librarians Society of North America, "New and Revised LC Subject Headings," *ARLIS/NA Update,* 4 (1993).

Belanger, Terry, *The Rare Book School 1991 Yearbook* (New York: Book Arts Press, 1991).

Bibliographic Standards Committee, *Genre Terms: A Thesaurus for Use in Rare Book and Special Collections Cataloging* (Chicago: ALA, 1983).

Bibliographic Standards Committee. *Printing and Publishing Evidence Thesauri for Use in Rare Book and Special Collections Cataloging* (Chicago: ALA, 1986).

Crawford, Walt, *MARC, for Library Use.* (White Plains: Knowledge Industries, 1984).

Cummings, Anthony M. *University Libraries and Scholarly Communication: A Study Prepared for The Andrew W. Mellon Foundation* (S.l.: Association of Research Libraries, 1992)

Haas, Walter J., *The National Coordinated Cataloging Program: An Assessment of the Pilot Project.* (Washingon, D.C.: Council on Library Resources, 1990), Preface.

Library of Congress, *Cataloging Service Bulletin* 36 (1993).

Library of Congress, *Subject Headings* (Washington, D.C.: Library of Congress, 1986).

Library of Congress, *Subject Headings* (Washington, D.C.: Library of Congress, 1993).

Parker, Elisabeth Betz, *LC Thesaurus for Graphic Materials: Topical Terms for Subject Access* (Washington, D.C.: Library of Congress, 1987).

Research Libraries Group, Inc., Mid-Decade Planning Group, *First Report* (Stanford, Ca.: RLG, 1993).

Zinkham, Helena and Elisabeth Betz Parker, *Descriptive Terms for Graphic Materials: Genre and Physical Characteristic Headings* (Washington, D.C.: Library of Congress, 1986).

NOTES

1. Walter J. Haas, *The National Coordinated Cataloging Program: An Assessment of the Pilot Project* (Washington, D.C.: Council on Library Resources, 1990), p. v.
2. "The Ohio College Library Center, now the Online Computer Library Center, was founded in 1967, though provision of online services did not begin until 1971. At Stanford, Project BALLOTS (Bibliographic Automation of Large Library Operations Using a Time-Sharing System) also began in 1967; the project eventually resulted in an online multi-library network in the 1970s, and was transformed in the Research Libraries Information Network (RLIN) at the end of the decade." Walt Crawford, *MARC, for Library Use* (White Plains: Knowledge Industries, 1984), p. 18.
3. Library of Congress, **Subject Headings** (Washington, D.C.: Library of Congress, 1993), p. iii.
4. The Independent Research Libraries Association's *Proposals for Establishing Standards for the Cataloguing of Rare Books and Specialized Research Materials in Machine-readable Form.*
5. American National Standards Institute, *Guidelines for Thesaurus Structure, Construction, and Use: Approved June 30, 1980* (New York, 1980).
6. The IRLA Proposal influenced the Bibliographic Standards Committee agenda for the next seven years. Between 1983 and 1990, The Committee published five more thesauri, Its *Printing and Publishing Evidence Thesaurus*, two thesauri neatly spliced together, followed *Genre Terms: A Thesaurus*, in turn to be followed by *Provenance Evidence: A Thesaurus* (1988), *Binding Terms: a Thesaurus* (1988), *Paper Terms: A Thesaurus* (1990) and *Type Evidence: A Thesaurus* (1990).
7. In February and then May.
8. Proposal 82-21.
9. So much so, in fact the idea of combining material now coded as 755 into 655 was briefly considered and abandoned.
10. Helena Zinkham and Elisabeth Betz Parker, *Descriptive Terms for Graphic Materials: Genre and Physical Characteristic Headings* (Washington, D.C.: Library of Congress, 1986), p. vi.
11. *Ibid.*, p. v.
12. *Ibid.*, p. xii.
13. *Ibid.*
14. *Ibid.*, p. 129.
15. *Ibid.*, p. 115.
16. Elisabeth Betz Parker, *LC Thesaurus for Graphic Materials, Topical Terms for Subject Access* (Washington, D.C., Library of Congress, 1987), p. v.
17. *Art and Architecture Thesaurus* (Williamstown, Mass.: Getty Art History Information Program, 1987)
18. Parker, p. viii.
19. *Ibid.*
20. Nonetheless, *LCTGM* continues to provide useful service to academic and research libraries and, as of 8 August, 1993, the Library of Congress has plans to issue an updated edition.
21. *Art and Architecture Thesaurus*, p. 5.
22. *Ibid.* p. 39.
23. Facets have also been defined as "mutually exclusive categories of information describing an object or situation" (MARBI 88-10 3).
24. *Art and Architecture Thesaurus*, p. 45.
25. *Ibid.*, p. 41.
26. *Ibid.*, p. 27.
27. *Ibid.*, p. 28.
28. As of 1990 publication.
29. The *AAT User Survey* found that 13% of the respondents felt they would like to see "Styles and Periods" more fully developed, a measure of dissatisfaction inspired by no other facet.
30. *Art and Architecture Thesaurus*, p. 28.

31. *Ibid.*
32. *Ibid.*
33. *Ibid.*
34. *Ibid.*
35. *Ibid.*
36. *Ibid*, p. 6-7.
37. The MARC bibliographic field for Faceted Topical Terms, 654, was created to contain a topical subject created from a faceted vocabulary. "For each term found in the field, an identification is given as to the facet/hierarchy in the thesaurus from which the term came. In addition, identification is given as to which terms is the focus terms of the expression. *A field may contain more than one expression*" (MARBI Proposal no. 93-6).
38. Alfred Willis, "AAT Update," *ARLIS/NA Update*, No. 4 (1993), p. 3.
39. *Ibid.*, p. 3-4.
40. Explanations for not using the *AAT* cited by respondents in the survey include costliness (11.9%), lack of training (8.9%) and using another vocabulary (15.1%).
41. Cummings, Anthony M. *University Libraries and Scholarly Communication: A Study Prepared for The Andrew W. Mellon Foundation* (S.l.: Association of Research Libraries, 1992), p. 23.
42. Research Libraries Group, Inc., Mid-Decade Planning Group, *First Report.* (Stanford, Ca.: RLG, 1993), p. 3.
43. Terry Belanger, *The Rare Book School 1991 Yearbook* (New York Book Arts Press, 1991), p. 89.

Processing and Cataloging of Archival Photograph Collections

by Jackie M. Dooley

Archival photograph collections are as diverse as the available methodologies for processing and cataloging them, and there is not one approach that will work in every environment. Archives, libraries, museums, and other specialized institutions all have different traditions and standards (or a lack thereof) for dealing with photographic collections. This paper therefore does not prescribe one particular methodology, but rather presents a sampler of some of the problems that are likely to be encountered in any environment, some solutions that are available, and essential steps that curators, catalogers, and administrators might take in their own institutional contexts before deciding on a method for processing and cataloging archival photographic collections. The paper principally addresses a context in which traditional archival control is used for processing and in which library-based standards are used for creation of catalog records.

Photographs, like most special format materials, can be very intimidating to the non-specialist who is forced to deal with them simply because his institution owns them and there is no photography specialist. And like other special materials, it is imperative that staff learn something about them if they are to care for the materials well and insure their long-term survival. A variety of excellent basic sources are available for acquainting oneself with the history, identification, care, and preservation of historic photographs (see Bibliography).

The *Processing* issues addressed are: Identifying the nature and purpose of a collection; the Limitations of original order for photograph collections; and Control of negatives and transparencies. The *Cataloging* topics are: the Myth of the need for item-level records; Choice of cataloging code and USMARC format; Choice of main entry; Some authority work problems;

and Choice of a subject thesaurus. Lastly, some available professional development opportunities for photograph curators and catalogers are described.

PROCESSING ISSUES

Identifying the Nature and Purpose of a Collection

As with any other archival material, it is difficult to set in place an appropriate processing program for photograph collections until one explicitly comes to terms with the scope of what the institution has, and why. In the not atypical situation of a repository that has never gained control of its photographic holdings, it is wise to conduct an overall inventory as a first step in order to appraise and quantify existing holdings. By gathering data concerning the subject matter, photographic processes, and film sizes represented in the collection, and in what quantities, prior to undertaking specific processing projects, it becomes possible to set in place a sensible overall processing program.

For example, knowing the range of film types and sizes represented in negative collections makes it possible to establish a repository-wide numbering system that will stand the test of time, as well as to make efficient decisions concerning the types and quantities of storage containers necessary to house these materials safely in isolation from other media. Discovering sooner rather than later whether the collection includes nitrate or acetate negatives will quite simply dictate whether these materials survive at all. Obtaining at least a rough sense as to whether or not particular negatives have corresponding prints is critical for determining the extent to which the collections will be publicly serviceable until the institution can afford to make additional prints. And as with any special collection, identifying existing subject strengths enables staff to plan appropriate grant writing and fund raising campaigns, not to mention sensible directions for cataloging and collection development.

Information gathered about the origins and nature of the images themselves will help determine what will be necessary to catalog the collections adequately. Do the collections consist largely of modern silver gelatin prints that call for no special access by process and technique, or are there a variety of nineteenth-century processes, cased images, card photographs, and photomechanical images that may invite study or exhibition as artifacts in addition to their subject content? Are the images strictly documentary and by amateur photographers, or will it be necessary to invest in a library of photography reference sources sufficient to identify a range of professional photographers whose work might have artistic or monetary value matching or exceeding the images' apparent documentary importance? Are most images sufficiently identified by association with the textual archival materials with which they were acquired, or is the institution faced with numerous isolated, uncaptioned images that will require considerable historical research to identify?

The Limitations of Original Order for Photograph Collections

Basic archival principles call for maintaining, whenever possible, the original order in which materials were acquired in order not to lose the meaning of the context in which they were created. With photographs, however, original order is frequently irrelevant or not useful. For example, many collections of photographic prints are acquired in total chaos, rendering original order virtually irrelevant. If prints and their corresponding negatives are acquired together, the prints may or may not be received in an order that is conducive to research; if not, they should be rearranged. Negatives are often acquired interfiled with textual manuscripts and other media, and they must be removed and isolated for preservation reasons. If a collection of unprinted negatives is acquired, the negatives can be numbered and maintained in original order. When prints are made, the prints can be arranged in whatever order is appropriate for ease of use; there is no need whatsoever to maintain prints in the same order as negatives.

If small lots of images are acquired piecemeal, and the images have no particular known provenance or integrity as a group, they can be incorporated into made-up groupings with other materials so acquired and arranged in a useful order, such as by format and/or subject. The Getty Center, for example, acquires large numbers of architectural images in this way and groups them first by format (such as stereographs, postcards, or loose prints) for ease of storage, and second by hierarchical geographic location for ease of research access. Images of international expositions, an area in which the Center's collecting is particularly intense, are arranged by city and exposition name to match the approach usually taken in published sources. On the other hand, the Center's Andreas Brown Collection of ca. 10,000 photographic postcards is maintained intact due to provenance, but it has been arranged in a useful subject order for browsing.

Control of Negatives and Transparencies

Collections of film-based materials, particularly large collections, can be particularly intimidating. They are difficult to handle, easy to damage, expensive to duplicate, have a habit of becoming permanently disassociated from their corresponding prints, and perhaps worst of all, conservation research increasingly shows that most negatives and transparencies will self destruct over time unless stored under prohibitively expensive controlled environmental conditions.[1]

At least some of these horrors can be mitigated, however, by setting in place a straightforward methodology for controlling negatives and transparencies. Key elements of such a system include establishing an in-house numbering system to organize and store them by collection and by size, matching corresponding prints to negatives whenever feasible and recording the negative number on the verso of each print, keeping careful records as to which negatives lack prints, and, whenever possible, withholding original negatives from use by researchers.

Preservation of negatives and transparencies is undeniably complex, and there is little value in collecting them at all if an institution lacks the resources to properly care for them. Acetate and nitrate film *will* physically deteriorate to the point of total destruction, and color film *will* fade and discolor over the not-so-long term if not kept in a stable environment with cool temperatures and low humidity (the recommended temperature and humidity levels vary depending on the type of film; 40 degrees of temperature and 40 percent humidity seems to be an acceptable compromise when a variety of materials will be stored in the same environment). These preservation issues are emphasized simply as a curatorial alert: an institution should not purchase negatives or transparencies or accept them as gifts unless the staff is willing to learn what they have and to give the materials the care they require.

CATALOGING ISSUES

The Myth of the Need for Item-Level Records

One often hears it stated that photographs require item-level cataloging if they are to be made adequately accessible to researchers. It seems likely that this notion intimidates many repositories from tackling their photograph backlogs at all, and it particularly seems to be a factor currently inhibiting institutions from undertaking digital imaging projects. The practice of calendaring manuscripts has been put to rest by archivists who confronted the fact that item-level description was both insupportably expensive and unnecessary. Item-level records for most archival photograph collections must similarly be recognized as another relic of a more leisurely past.

By arranging related images, be they originals or digital surrogates, in a useful browseable sequence, the sort of group-level or folder-level description typically provided for textual archival materials can be equally successful for many archival image collections. In a newspaper photo morgue, for example, multiple rolls of film typically document the same event, and once the event and its participants have been identified, even item-level photo captions may be unnecessary. In a collection of architectural images of a building taken by a particular photographer at one point in time, a single catalog record could describe the overall project, while detail-specific captions, and perhaps also subject tracings, might well suffice to identify particular images. In a non-museum setting, it is the unusual collection that contains many photographs so dissimilar from all others, or so significant as individual items, that full item-level cataloging is truly necessary.

The Research Libraries Group (RLG) Digital Image Access Project, in which the Getty Center and seven other RLG institutions are participants, seeks to test a variety of issues related to description and access for digitized photographic collections.[2] One of the key points being addressed is that of the one-to-one correspondence of catalog record to digitized image that has been implemented in most imaging projects to date. The project will demonstrate two approaches for hierarchical linking of images to both collection-level catalog records and archival finding aids without sacrificing the viewer's understanding of the relationship between description and image.[3] Given that cataloging has proven to be the most time-consuming, and therefore the most expensive, aspect of many digitization projects, crossing this hurdle could help make imaging a viable option for many more photographic archives.[4]

Choice of Cataloging Code and USMARC Format

Two different cataloging codes for describing archival materials in a manner compatible with library cataloging are in widespread use by photographic archives: these are *Graphic Materials*, written by Elisabeth Betz and published by the Library of Congress,[5] and *Archives, Personal Papers, and Manuscripts*, written by Steven Hensen and published by the Society of American Archivists.[6] In direct parallel, two USMARC formats also exist: the Visual Materials Format (VIM) and the Archives and Manuscripts Control format (AMC).[7] How should an archives choose which rules and format to use to catalog its photograph collections?

Graphic Materials was written for the express purpose of cataloging archival still pictures, both single items and collections, and its extremely specific rules of description make it the best choice for an archive specializing in image collections that wishes to use the USMARC format and incorporate its records into a standard library catalog. The rules on devising content-oriented titles and on preparing physical descriptions are among the most useful aspects of *Graphic Materials*, as they are so specifically geared to the situations encountered in cataloging various types of still images. *Graphic Materials* addresses both published and unpublished images in order to accommodate the voluminous stereographs, travel views, postcards, lithographs, and other published images sold in great volume in the nineteenth and early twentieth centuries.

Archives, Personal Papers, and Manuscripts (APPM), on the other hand, was written to encompass the generic needs of a wide range of archival repositories regardless of the particular archival media they hold. It does not, however, contain any specific advice to address the particular characteristics of visual materials, sound recordings, electronic records, or any other special media; APPM examples illustrate either explicitly textual materials or generic collections of "records" or "papers" without mention of particular media. An archive desiring, for example, to describe in a standard way the specific photographic media contained in a collection will receive no help in doing so from APPM. Similarly, an archive that is building subject-oriented collections from related acquisitions would find no advice in APPM on devising meaningful titles. APPM does not address published materials at all, and so no guidance is given for transcribing the data printed on published original photographs, including titles, statements of responsibility, or series titles and numbering . APPM can be used to describe images, but the resulting description is likely to be more generic than a description created by following *Graphic Materials*.

An institution's use of a particular USMARC format is usually in parallel with its choice of cataloging code. In other words, users of *Graphic Materials* tend to use the VIM format, while users of APPM use the AMC format. This is not strictly or necessarily true, but it is the norm. The two formats vary in fewer significant ways than do the cataloging rules themselves, since the formats simply define data categories or elements while the rules more specifically define the content of each element. The VIM format includes many fixed field elements designed to facilitate identification and retrieval of specific characteristics of visual media, while AMC's fixed field is simpler and more generic. AMC includes a number of note fields not found in VIM, but the same data could easily be coded in VIM records in a general note field, and in any event, these differences will disappear when USMARC format integration is implemented.

Many archives use APPM to describe photographs and other image collections for pragmatic reasons. There may be a feeling that training staff in use of a second cataloging manual would be too time consuming, or because the AMC database software being used does not accommodate VIM, or because of a desire to house all archival records in the same RLIN file.

Regarding the first concern (the training issue), the two codes are in fact remarkably harmonious, and a cataloger familiar with APPM will find it quite easy to use *Graphic Materials* when its specific guidance is necessary. As for the second issue (software limitations), repositories should consider at least following the advice provided by *Graphic Materials* to create more useful physical descriptions and titles for photograph collections, since this is possible regardless of the software being used. As USMARC format integration is implemented, one hopes that the vendors of microcomputer-based archival cataloging software will enhance their systems to accommodate the full integrated format. The third concern (separate RLIN files) deserves little sympathy, not only because searching across files is so simple in RLIN, but also because storing visual materials records in a file other than VIM is a disservice to researchers who are using the database to locate archival photographs and other visual materials.[8]

Marion Matters has written an excellent article comparing the various cataloging codes used by archival repositories, particularly *Graphic Materials* and APPM, in several additional areas[9]. Similar issues were explored in a seminar session at the Society of American Archivists conference in New Orleans in September 1993 at which three speakers discussed the relative merits of APPM, *Graphic Materials*, and a third set of archival cataloging rules, *Archival Moving Image Materials*.[10] One might hope that SAA endorsement of the latter two codes will emerge from an open discussion of their specific merits for cataloging visual materials.[11]

Choice of Main Entry

Graphic Materials does not include rules for selecting or formulating a main entry or other access points. Catalogers are directed to follow the *Anglo-American Cataloguing Rules*, 2nd edition (AACR2).[12] As the Library of Congress' own pictorial catalogers have since realized, however, AACR2 is heavily biased toward "authorship" of texts and leads to some highly unsatisfactory results when cataloging photographs.[13]

Perhaps the most significant problem relates to corporate authorship, defined narrowly in AACR2 as being limited to publications that either are "those of an administrative nature dealing with the corporate body itself," or "those that record the collective thought of the body" (AACR2 21.1B2) . This is extremely unhelpful in cataloging photographs . What, for example, does a portrait of an individual artist in her studio taken by the New York firm of Peter A. Juley & Son have to do with the "administrative nature" or "collective thought" of Juley & Son? The answer is nothing. A cataloger following AACR2 would therefore enter such an image under title, which in the case of such a photograph, generally means a title devised by the cataloger. If, on the other hand, the particular Juley staff member who took the photograph were known, AACR2's rule on single personal authorship could be applied; unfortunately, the particular photographer seldom is known, and in any case, the firm's role is probably far more significant. And what about a large collection of Juley & Son photographs, or perhaps the firm's entire archive?

One might be able to stretch a corporate main entry out of AACR2, particularly for a record describing the full Juley & Son archive containing correspondence and financial records in addition to photographs. It would be preferable, however, if catalogers did not have to perform complex mental gymnastics in order to achieve useful results, particularly when the work of so many special materials catalogers is scrutinized by central cataloging departments somewhat unsympathetic to the unusual characteristics of so-called "non-book formats".

The guidance given in APPM is far more useful, albeit not specifically focused on the situations that arise in cataloging photographs. For the full Juley archive, APPM would definitely call for a corporate main entry; for the individual photograph, the situation is less clear . APPM's intrinsic focus on "provenance" rather than "authorship" would very likely lead to a corporate main entry for the single photograph as well, since the firm, as the employer of various photographers hired to photograph various artists and the contents of their studios, is more chiefly responsible for the creation of the photograph than is the specific staff photographer.

In any event, interested catalogers should be lobbying LC's Prints and Photographs Division to add rules for choice of entry to any future edition of *Graphic Materials*. Such rules undoubtedly would be based in part on the useful precedent established by APPM.

Some Authority Work Problems

Photographers are woefully under-represented in the Library of Congress Name Authority File.[14] Photograph catalogers must therefore do a great deal of original authority work, just like other archival catalogers. Fortunately, a number of excellent reference sources exist for identifying photographers, including the *George Eastman House Photographers Biography File*[15] and Edwards' *International Guide to Nineteenth-Century Photographers and Their Works*.[16]

Formulating an AACR2-compatible form of name can be tricky for some photographers. This is particularly true when their names appear on card mounts or in negatives in a variety of forms, some of which appear to constitute personal names, while others have the appearance of corporate names. Names of partners come and go with alarming frequency, and tracing the history of a firm in order to determine when a new "corporate body" was born is generally either impossible or too potentially time consuming to contemplate. Catalogers are on their own in this rather uncharted territory and must seek practical solutions. At the Getty Center, for example, the technique of making "see also" references between personal names of photographers and the firms in which their names appear as partners is used in order to forge a link between photographers' personal and corporate works.

Choice of Subject Thesaurus

The importance of subject indexing for photograph collections is indisputable, and for any collection containing a variety of forms of material and photographic processes, access to these attributes is also of considerable significance.

General photographic archives have, at minimum, three thesauri or subject heading lists to choose from for indexing these types of terminology: the *Library of Congress Subject Headings*[17] and the *Art and Architecture Thesaurus*[18] both contain terms for indexing subjects, forms, and processes, while LC's Prints and Photographs Division utilizes two separate thesauri: the *LC Thesaurus for Graphic Materials*[19] for subjects and *Descriptive Terms for Graphic Materials*[20] for forms and processes. How do these lists differ, how are they similar, and how is a photographic archives to choose the "best" one for its purposes? First, a brief summary of the scope and purpose of each publication.

Library of Congress Subject Headings (LCSH) is a massive general subject heading list constructed principally via indexing of the unparalleled book collections of the Library of Congress. For any general topic, the array of terms, both abstract and concrete, simple and complex, is staggering. LC itself uses LCSH primarily for indexing subjects per se (in USMARC field 650). LCSH also is authorized for use in USMARC field 655 (Form/Genre), however, and it contains a surprising number of form and genre terms. Such terms are used in some cases for indexing the subject content, and in other cases the form, of published book materials. LCSH is weak in terms describing photographic forms and processes, however, presumably because few monographs have been written about specific ones.

The *Art and Architecture Thesaurus* (AAT) was designed, as its title indicates, to index art and architecture materials, and is intended to be useable with materials in any original medium, from books to photographs to slide reproductions to three-dimensional works of art. AAT is meant to be conceptually comprehensive in the areas within its scope; it does not spring from the indexing of a particular collection of materials, as does LCSH. AAT is constructed of separate hierarchies containing simple concepts intended to be post-coordinated by the indexer into complex headings; some of these hierarchies are Visual Works (which includes photographic terminology), Drawings, Built Complexes, Building Divisions and Site Elements, Styles and Periods, People and Organizations, Functions, and Information Forms. Despite its seemingly limited scope, AAT has proven remarkably versatile for indexing a broad variety of textual archival materials; several hierarchies were in fact constructed in close collaboration with archivists.

The two graphic materials thesauri published by the Library of Congress, the *LC Thesaurus for Graphic Materials* (TGM) and *Descriptive Terms for Graphic Materials*, were designed specifically for indexing the archival still picture collections of the Library of Congress. The compilers of these thesauri have striven to use terminology consistent with LCSH and AAT in areas where their scopes overlap, but the inherently distinct nature of the various lists can render quite different results. Since it was designed solely for picture indexing, TGM tends to express concepts in simple, concrete terms. It does not, for example, contain terms such as "Architecture, Domestic" or "Architecture, Ecclesiastical" as found in LCSH, but rather the more concrete "Dwellings" and other specific building types, such as "Churches", "Barns", and "Courthouses". Also, TGM includes terms such as "Children playing outdoors", "Hayrides", and "Ice sculptures" that are not in LCSH because they are not the subjects of entire books, and that are not in AAT because they fall outside the scope of art, architecture, and the supporting hierarchies.[21]

Descriptive Terms for Graphic Materials (GMGPC), the thesaurus for indexing photographic forms and processes, contains roughly the same number of photography concepts found in the AAT, but the particular terms found in each are surprisingly different. Also, whereas GMGPC terms are fixed in the thesaurus, the use of post-coordination by an AAT indexer can easily result in AAT headings that express either greater or lesser specificity, or that are quite different in construction, from the corresponding GMGPC terms. For example, from AAT, one could construct "Hand-colored albumen prints", while GMGPC would render "Albumen prints—Color".[22] GMGPC has "Portrait photographs" and "Daguerreotypes" as separate terms; from AAT, one could construct "Portrait daguerreotypes", or perhaps "Daguerreotype portraits", or maintain the separate terms "Daguereretypes" and "Portraits", and so on.

How to choose a thesaurus? Rather than blindly adopting someone else's opinion or falling back on popular platitudes about a particular list's virtues or vices, each institution should experiment with the vocabularies under consideration. A cataloger should try indexing her photograph collection using, for example, LCSH and TGM, and compare the results. If TGM seems easier and more specific for indexing photographs, compare the results with LCSH in terms of whether the resulting headings are sufficiently compatible; this compatibility, or lack thereof, will be significant in terms of researcher convenience in a library catalog that integrates books, photographs, and other materials. If photographs will be indexed only very broadly within the context of textual archival collections, TGM's specificity is probably unnecessary. For an institution principally interested in a thesaurus for indexing photographic forms and processes, LCSH lacks the necessary terminology and therefore will not suffice; in such a situation, TGM should be compared with AAT in terms of ease of use, the headings each delivers, and comprehensiveness.

PROFESSIONAL DEVELOPMENT OPPORTUNITIES

A variety of professional development opportunities exist for those interested in developing expertise in photograph processing and cataloging.

Considerable activity is concentrated under the auspices of the Society of American Archivists, and membership in the Society is highly recommended for those for whose professional responsibilities are significantly comprised of work with archival photograph collections. SAA includes two groups devoted to images: the Visual Materials Section, which publishes a newsletter titled *Views* and is extremely active in developing programs and tours for the annual conference held each autumn, and the MARC-VM Roundtable, which holds open discussions of image cataloging issues at the annual conference. SAA also sponsors a highly regarded workshop on management of photographic collections; this workshop usually is held at least twice each year, and SAA is diligent about moving its workshops to different sites throughout the country in order to facilitate broad participation.[23]

ACRL's Rare Books and Manuscripts Section is less specifically focused on archival materials than is SAA, but discussions of issues related to photograph collections are sometimes held by the Manuscripts and Other Formats Discussion Group. Also, the Bibliographic Standards Committee has discussed sponsoring a seminar on image cataloging for a future RBMS preconference.[24]

For slide librarians and art-oriented photo specialists, the Visual Resources Association is an important professional association. VRA sponsors an annual conference (usually held in proximity to that of the College Art Association), publishes a *Bulletin* and the journal *Visual Resources*, and has a Data Standards Committee whose work is of particular interest to image catalogers.[25]

The Getty Conservation Institute in Marina del Rey, California, annually sponsors two one-week workshops devoted to the subject of photo conservation and preservation. The principal instructor is Debbie Hess Norris of the University of Delaware and the Winterthur Museum, whose knowledge of photographic conservation and whose teaching abilities are legendary. Only about twelve students are accepted for each course, so competition is somewhat fierce, but for those accepted the course is free. Although these courses are explicitly focused on preservation, the value of such information for processing archivists is obvious.[26]

Lastly, electronic mail bulletin boards have emerged in the past several years as a significant source of professional dialogue and information, particularly for those who cannot travel to conferences. Four lists of potential interest for photography catalogers are PHOTOHST (history of photography), ARCHIVES (general issues of interest to archivists), LCSH-AMC (use of *Library of Congress Subject Headings* in archival cataloging), and VRA-L (sponsored by the Visual Resources Association).[27]

In conclusion, processing and cataloging of archival photograph collections is a complex enterprise that requires at least the same levels of creativity and tolerance for ambiguity as any other archival activity. Once sampled, however, it is a most addictive and rewarding professional endeavor.

PROCESSING AND CATALOGING OF ARCHIVAL PHOTOGRAPH COLLECTIONS: A SELECTIVE BIBLIOGRAPHY

Curatorship, Identification, Preservation

Archival Storage of Photographic Materials (Syracuse, NY: Gaylord, 1994) (Gaylord Preservation Pathfinder no. 3).

A clear and concise summary of basic storage and housing issues and solutions.

Baldwin, Gordon, *Looking at Photographs: A Guide to Technical Terms* (Malibu, CA: The J. Paul Getty Museum, in association with British Museum Press, 1991), 88 p.

Contains concise narrative explanations of 101 photographic terms, including 63 with accompanying illustrations (some in color). An excellent source for basic historical and technical terminology. (Available from: The J. Paul Getty Museum, 17985 Pacific Coast Highway, Malibu, CA 90265-5799.)

Newhall, Beaumont, *The History of Photography: From 1839 to the Present*, Completely rev. and enl. ed. (New York: Museum of Modern Art; Boston: Distributed by New York Graphic Society Books, 1982). 319 p.

An excellent brief history by the "father" of the study of the history of photography.

Porro, Jennifer, ed., *Photograph Preservation and the Research Library* (Mountain View, CA: The Research Libraries Group, Inc., 1991), 56 p.

Papers presented at RLG's symposium on the preservation of photo collections in research libraries held in October 1990. Includes useful essays on preservation planning, duplication options for deteriorating negatives, bibliographic control and access, and other topics.

Reilly, James M., *Care and Identification of 19th-Century Photographic Prints* (Rochester, NY: Eastman Kodak Company, 1986. (KODAK Publication no. G-2S), 116 p.

A superb source for advice concerning identification, storage, housing, and preservation of nineteenth-century prints. Includes a fold-out chart illustrating processes under magnification.

Reilly, James M., *IPI Storage Guide for Acetate Film* (Rochester, NY: Image Permanence Institute, Rochester Institute of Technology, 1993).

The latest guidance on the storage conditions necessary to extend the life of acetate film materials.

Ritzenthaler, Mary Lynn et al., *Administration of Photographic Collections* (Chicago, IL: Society of American Archivists, 1985). 2nd printing. (SAA Basic Manual Series), 173 p.

Includes chapters on photographic processes, appraisal and collecting, arrangement and description, preservation, legal issues, and managing a copy service. (Available from: Society of American Archivists, 600 S. Federal St., Suite 504, Chicago, IL 60605.

Wilhelm, Henry and Carol Brower, *The Permanence and Care of Color Photographs: Traditional and Digital Color Prints, Color Negatives, Slides, and*

Motion Pictures (Grinnell, Iowa: Preservation Publishing Company, 1993), 742 p.

Authority Work Sources

International Museum of Photography at George Eastman House, *George Eastman House Photographers Biography File* (Rochester, NY: George Eastman House).
    Microfiche edition; available by subscription. Also available online.

Edwards, Gary, *International Guide to Nineteenth-Century Photographers and Their Works: Based on Catalogues of Auction Houses and Dealers* (Boston, Mass.: G.K. Hall, 1988). 591 p.

Library of Congres, *Name Authorities Cumulative Microform* (Washington, D.C.: Library of Congress, 1977-).
    Also available online via OCLC, RLIN, and other bibliographic utilities or systems.

Researching Photographers (Tucson, Arizona: Center for Creative Photography, Univ. of Arizona, 1984). 15 p.

Rudisill, Richard et al., *Photographers: A Sourcebook for Historical Research* (Brownsville, CA: Carl Mautz Publishing, 1991). 103 p.

Cataloging Tools

The Art and Architecture Thesaurus, Toni Petersen, ed. (New York: Oxford University Press, 2nd ed., 1994). "Published on behalf of The Getty Art History Information Program."
    A hierarchical thesaurus intended for indexing materials in all formats related to the subjects of art and architecture, the AAT has proven its versatility for indexing archival materials as well. Application guidelines for cataloging books, visual materials, and archival materials were issued with the 2nd ed. of the AAT. (Available from: Oxford University Press, Humanities and Social Sciences Marketing, 200 Madison Ave., New York, N.Y. 10157-0913. Available in both print and electronic forms, and online via RLIN.)

Betz, Elisabeth W., *Graphic Materials: Rules for Describing Original Items and Historical Collections* (Washington, D.C.: Library of Congress, 1982). 155 p.
    The Library of Congress cataloging code for archival visual materials, including both published and unpublished photographs. Contains particularly useful advice on devising titles for collections and for

recording the physical descriptions of various photographic media. (Available from: Cataloging Distribution Service, Library of Congress, Washington, D.C. 20540.)

Betz, Elisabeth W., *LC Thesaurus for Graphic Materials: Topical Terms for Subject Access* (Washington, D.C.: Library of Congress, 1987). 591 p.

The LC thesaurus for indexing the subject content of images in USMARC field 650. (Available from: Cataloging Distribution Service, Library of Congress, Washington, D.C. 20540.)

Hensen, Steven L., *Archives, Personal Papers, and Manuscripts* (Chicago, IL: The Society of American Archivists, 1989). 2nd ed. 196 p.

The rules endorsed by SAA for cataloging archival collections. Has no specific guidance for special materials such as photographs, but images can be accommodated in collection-level cataloging using APPM's generic approach. (Available from: Society of American Archivists, 600 S. Federal St., Suite 504, Chicago, IL 60605.)

Library of Congress, Subject Cataloging Division, *Library of Congress Subject Headings* (Washington, D.C.: Library of Congress).

Available in print, microfiche, and online editions.

Zinkham, Helena, and Elisabeth Betz Parker, *Descriptive Terms for Graphic Materials: Genre and Physical Characteristics Headings* (Washington, D.C.: Library of Congress, 1986). 135 p.

The LC thesaurus for indexing forms, genres, and physical characteristics of visual materials in USMARC fields 655 and 755. (Available from: Cataloging Distribution Service, Library of Congress, Washington, D.C. 20540.)

Cataloging Theory and Practice

Dooley, Jackie M. and Helena Zinkham, "The Object as 'Subject': Providing Address to Genres, Forms of Materials, and Physical Characteristics." In: *Beyond the Book: Extending MARC for Subject Access*, ed. by Toni Petersen and Pat Molholt (Boston, Mass.: G.K. Hall, 1990), pp. 43–80.

Evans, Linda J. and Maureen O'Brien Will., *MARC for Visual Materials: A Compendium of Practice* (Chicago, IL: The Chicago Historical Society 1988). 424 p.

Greenberg, Jane., "Intellectual Control of Visual Archives: A Comparison between the *Art and Architecture Thesaurus* and the *Library of Congress Thesaurus for Graphic Materials*." *Cataloging & Classification Quarterly*, 16:1 (1993), pp. 85–117.

Matters, Marion, "Reconciling Sibling Rivalry in the AACR2 'Family': The Potential for Agreement on Rules for Archival Description of All Types of Materials," *American Archivist*, 53 (1990), pp. 76–93.

Orbach, Barbara, "Integrating Concepts: Corporate Main Entry and Graphic Materials." *Cataloging & Classification Quarterly*, 8:2 (1987/88), pp. 71–89.

Orbach, Barbara, "So That Others May See: Tools for Cataloging Still Images." *Cataloging and Classification Quarterly*, 11:3/4 (1990), pp. 163–191.

Shatford, Sara, "Describing a Picture: A Thousand Words Are Seldom Cost Effective." *Cataloging and Classification Quarterly*, 4:4 (1984), pp. 13–30.

Shatford, Sara, "Analyzing the Subject of a Picture: A Theoretical Approach." *Cataloging and Classification Quarterly*, 6:3 (1986), pp. 39–62.

Yee, Martha, "Integration of Non-book Materials in AACR2." *Cataloging & Classification Quarterly*, 3:4 (1983), pp. 1–18.

NOTES

1. For specific information regarding storage conditions for acetate film materials, see: Reilly, James M., *IPI Storage Guide for Acetate Film* (Rochester, N.Y.: Image Permanence Institute, Richester Institute of Technology, 1993).

2. Contact: Linda West, Director of Member Services, The Research Libraries Group, 1200 Villa St., Mountain View, CA 94041-1100.

3. The approach for achieving this for archival finding aids is being developed by the Berkeley Finding Aid Project (funded by The U.S. Dept. of Education, Title II-A), which is developing a document type definition for SGML-based (Standard Generalized Mark-up Language) tagging of archival finding aids. Within this scenario, digitized image files can be linked to marked-up textual finding aids, as the Berkeley team will demonstrate as part of its participation in the RLG project. Contact: Daniel V. Pitti, The Library, UC Berkeley, Berkeley, CA 94720.

4. The approach taken by Columbia's Avery Library in the AVIADOR architectural drawings project, which also will be demonstrated within the context of the RLG project via Columbia's participation, utilizes group-level USMARC bibliographic records with item-level data coded in multiply-occurring 789 field (this is an RLIN MARC field that is not part of the USMARC format; it was presented to the MARBI committee as a discussion paper in June 1994.) Although a useful model for certain situations, even this approach to cataloging is too expensive for many extremely large documentary photograph collections.

5. Elisabeth W. Betz, *Graphic Materials: Rules for Describing Original Items and Historical Collections* (Washington, D.C.: Library of Congress, 1982).

6. S. L. Hensen, *Archives, Personal Papers, and Manuscripts* (Chicago, IL: The Society of American Archivists, 1989), 2nd ed.

7. Both the AMC and VIM formats are contained in: Library of Congress, *USMARC Format for Bibliographic Data: Including Guidelines for Content Designation* (Washinton, D.C.: Library of Congress, 1988), with updates.

8. In RLIN's new EUREKA search interface designed for end-user searching, all files are searched simultaneously unless the searcher specifies otherwise, which might seem to render this complaint irrelevant. Given the capability of many systems to allow users to explicitly limit a search by format of materials (manuscripts, visual materials, serials, books, etc.), however, it remains most useful in *any* system to code a record for the most appropriate format so that users will not miss relevant materials.

9. M. Matters, "Reconciling Sibling Rivalry in the AACR2 'Family': The Potential for Agreement on Rules for Archival Description of All Types of Materials," *American Archivist*, 53 (1990), pp. 76–93.

10. W. White-Hensen, *Archival Moving Image Materials: A Cataloging Manual* (Washington, D.C.: Motion Picture, Broadcasting and Recorded Sound Division, Library of Congress, 1984).

11. The three unpublished papers presented at the SAA seminar are: R. Pearce-Moses, "Round Pegs in Square Holes: Using Bibliographic Tools to Describe Archival Collections"; B. Carnell, "*Graphic Materials*: An APPM Alternative?"; and H. K. Mattoon, "Describing the Movies: AMIM, APPM, and AACR2."

12. *Anglo American Cataloguing Rules* (Chicago, IL: American Library Association, 1988), 2nd ed., revised.

13. See, for example: B. Orbach, "Integrating Concepts: Corporate Main Entry and Graphic Materials." *Cataloging & Classification Quarterly*, 8:2 (1987/88), pp. 71–89; M. Yee, "Integration of Non-book Materials in AACR2." *Cataloging & Classification Quarterly*, 3:4 (1983), pp. 1–18.

14. Library of Congress, *Name Authorities Cumulative Microform* (Washington, D.C.: Library of Congress, 1977–).

15. International Museum of Photography at George Eastman House, *George Eastman House Photographers Biography File*. Rochester, N.Y.: George Eastman House. This *Biography File* is now accessible through the Internet; See Andrew Eskind, "Photography Database Available on Internet," *Visual Resources*, X/2 (1994), pp. 119–127.

16. G. Edwards, *International Guide to Nineteenth-Century Photographers and Their Works: Based on Catalogues of Auction Houses and Dealers* (Boston, Mass.: G. K. Hall, 1988).

17. Library of Congress, Subject Cataloging Division, *Library of Congress Subject Headings* (Washington, D.C.: Library of Congress. 1993), 16th ed.

18. *The Art and Architecture Thesaurus*, Toni Petersen, ed. (New York: Oxford University Press, 2nd ed., 1994). "Published on behalf of The Getty Art History Information Program."

19. E. W. Betz, *LC Thesaurus for Graphic Materials: Topical Terms for Subject Access* (Washington, D.C: Library of Congress, 1987).

20. H. Zinkham and E. B. Parker, *Descriptive Terms for Graphic Materials: Genre and Physical Characteristics Headings* (Washington, D.C: Library of Congress, 1986).

21. For a more complete discussion of these issues, see: J. Greenberg, "Intellectual Control of Visual Archives: A Comparison between the *Art and Architecture Thesaurus* and the *Library of Congress Thesaurus for Graphic Materials*," *Cataloging & Classification Quarterly*, 16:1 (1993), pp. 85–117.

22. As published in GMGPC, the term would be "Albumen photoprints", but as of January 1993, the Prints and Photographs Division has eliminated its usage of "photoprints" in favor of "prints" in order to conform with both common usage and the *Art and Architecture Thesaurus*. See "Graphic Materials," *Cataloging Service Bulletin*, 60 (1993), pp. 53–54.

23. Contact the Society of American Archivists, 600 S. Federal St., Suite 504, Chicago, IL, 60605.

24. Contact the Association of College and Research Libraries, 50 E. Huron St., Chicago, IL 60611. Attn: Chair, Rare Books and Manuscripts Section.

25. Contact the Visual Resources Association, %Lynda White, University of Virginia, Fiske Kimball Fine Arts Library, Bayly Drive, Charlottesville, VA 22903.

26. Contact the Getty Conservation Institute, 4503 Glencoe Ave., Marina del Rey, CA 90292-7913.

27. As of June 1994, the Internet subscription address for each of these lists is as follows: PHOTOHST: listserv@asuvm.inre.asu.edu. ARCHIVES: listserv@arizvm1.ccit.arizona.edu. LCSH-AMC: listserv@asuvm.inre.asu.edu. VRA-L: listserv@uafsysb.uark.edu.

The Search for Ephemera Images

by William H. Helfand

Finding appropriate images for publication or for any other purpose has never been a simple task. The searcher must adopt a creative strategy to uncover the sought-for needle in the haystack, relying on collectors, libraries, museums, picture collections, books, and now videodiscs, CD-Roms, and electronic services. Even with crucial technological advances which have made recent searches productive, general difficulties remain, and there is no good substitute for lengthy experience. When specifications of form are added, requiring the searcher to find an image on, for example, a postcard, poster, caricature, broadside, or other form of printed ephemera, the effort becomes even more complex, for such ephemeral images are among the last to be individually cataloged in public collections, and aids to finding such images are scarce. Perhaps the best way to explore the means to deal with these complexities is to consider each of the possible sources: collectors, libraries, museums, and electronic media separately.

Collectors are a major source for images; in assembling their collections, they confront similar problems to the searcher. Consider the postcard collector as a model whose primary contact is with dealers at fairs and shows. The dealer accommodates the collector by arranging the stock of postcards in categories such as Advertising, Ships, Birds and Trains, separating groups by large dividing cards. But there is no universally accepted list of subjects, certainly no authority list, and the individual personality of the dealer dictates the designation to be used. One dealer's "Comics" is another dealer's "Humor." Medical subjects can be found under many more headings than those normally expected, such as Medicine, Health, Doctors, Dentists, Druggists, Nurses, Hospitals, Interiors, Shops or Drug Stores. There is not even universal agreement on whether the cards should be filed behind the dividing card or in front of it. Idiosyncrasy prevails. At times, a creative dealer will consider the plight of the searcher, and will provide a cross-reference, either by inserting a card to "see also," a photocopy of a postcard filed elsewhere or even a color-coded clip for other subjects, but such rewarding moments are exceptional and show no signs of increasing in number. The problems of the search of the postcard collector mirror those of all who seek appropriate images.

For the poster or caricature collector it is somewhat easier, for there are considerably fewer examples available and the search is a slower one. Here the knowledge of the collector is helpful in finding suitable images even when the dealer emphasizes that none are being offered. Most ephemera collectors depend on their own practiced eye, it being a rare experience to find a source of supply that provides easy subject access.

Collectors are not, as a rule, the first source to contact to locate an image. But they can often provide considerable help in the quest. Probably 80 to 90% of all cataloged ephemera collections are still in private hands, largely because libraries and museums have been slow to catalog their ephemera and to make their holdings available to researchers and scholars. In the field of postal history, for example, one recent author has estimated that 90% of all the objects that have been saved from destruction are still in private hands; undoubtedly this level will decrease as time goes on and public institutions further organize what they have.[1]

Since ephemera holdings are still largely in the hands of private collectors, access is not a simple matter. However, librarians, dealers, and membership lists published by organized ephemera collector's societies in the United States, England, Canada, France and now Australia and Norway, provide useful guides to locating collections. Invisible colleges have mushroomed, and collectors in varied fields of interest know colleagues who have additional holdings.[2] Some collectors will be found willing to provide images for researchers, at times for a fee, but others will be reluctant, at times vehemently, to do so. A major reason is often the compulsion to conceal availability of their materials for fear of potential thievery. Collectors have at times refused to join communities of like-minded individuals or have insisted that their names be kept out of published directories because of their apprehension.

Libraries, although also much concerned about thieves, are the source most frequently searched for ephemera images. Very few libraries, however, have properly organized their ephemera, frequently accumulating huge backlogs which appear to grow geometrically. If library backlogs could be considered as pyramids, books would be at the top, supported in sequence by serials, pamphlets and related literature, and finally ephemera at the bottom. The attention of catalogers would first be directed to the books at the top of the pyramid, but because of continually tightening limitations on library budgets and personnel, the prospects of getting to the ephemera at the bottom of the pile are rather slim. In some libraries it is doubtful that the ephemera will ever be made available to searchers. And, adding to the problem is the maxim that books may be finite, but ephemera is not, being almost infinite in its continual creation. Every day sees another batch of bus tickets produced and destroyed and, in some cases, saved. "How can we justify keeping these materials," lament many library directors, "if no one can find them and use them? It's hard to find a justification for maintaining backlogs of inaccessible materials in any institution that has a mission of serving its patrons, rather than simply preserving its collections untouched for some imagined future."[3]

If the uncataloged book is the unusable book, the uncataloged ephemera is lost to all. Because of this, it is perhaps better for the researcher if libraries were to provide minimal cataloging to get the essentials available, rather than to await the moment, which may never occur, when full cataloging can be carried out. A second alternative is for libraries to consider a two-step process with minimal efforts at first and full cataloging later. Of course, there is a belief among some catalogers that material difficult to find and keep need not be recorded, a pernicious attitude to anyone interested in ephemera.

A third possibility is to consider specific ephemera collections as an archive and to catalog the entire collection, rather than individual items. In 1992, the National Library of Medicine in Bethesda was given a collection of more than 1700 patent medicine almanacs, the majority from the second half of the nineteenth century. The collection has been cataloged once only, as a complete patent medicine almanac collection, and has quickly been made available to visiting researchers with finding lists by company and by images (more than 750) which have a medical subject. As is often the case with donations of ephemera collections, these finding lists were supplied by the donor, thereby saving the Library a considerable amount of work. To catalog each almanac would be a laborious task, but to consider the entire collection as a single item has enabled the NLM to provide access much more rapidly and inexpensively than by any alternative approach. (Figure 1)

An opposite cataloging decision has been reached by the College of Physicians of Philadelphia which was recently given a major collection of more than 12,000 medical, pharmaceutical, and dental bookplates which it is now cataloging. The College's labor-intensive effort to prepare a machine readable catalog of these bookplates will take considerable time, but will be

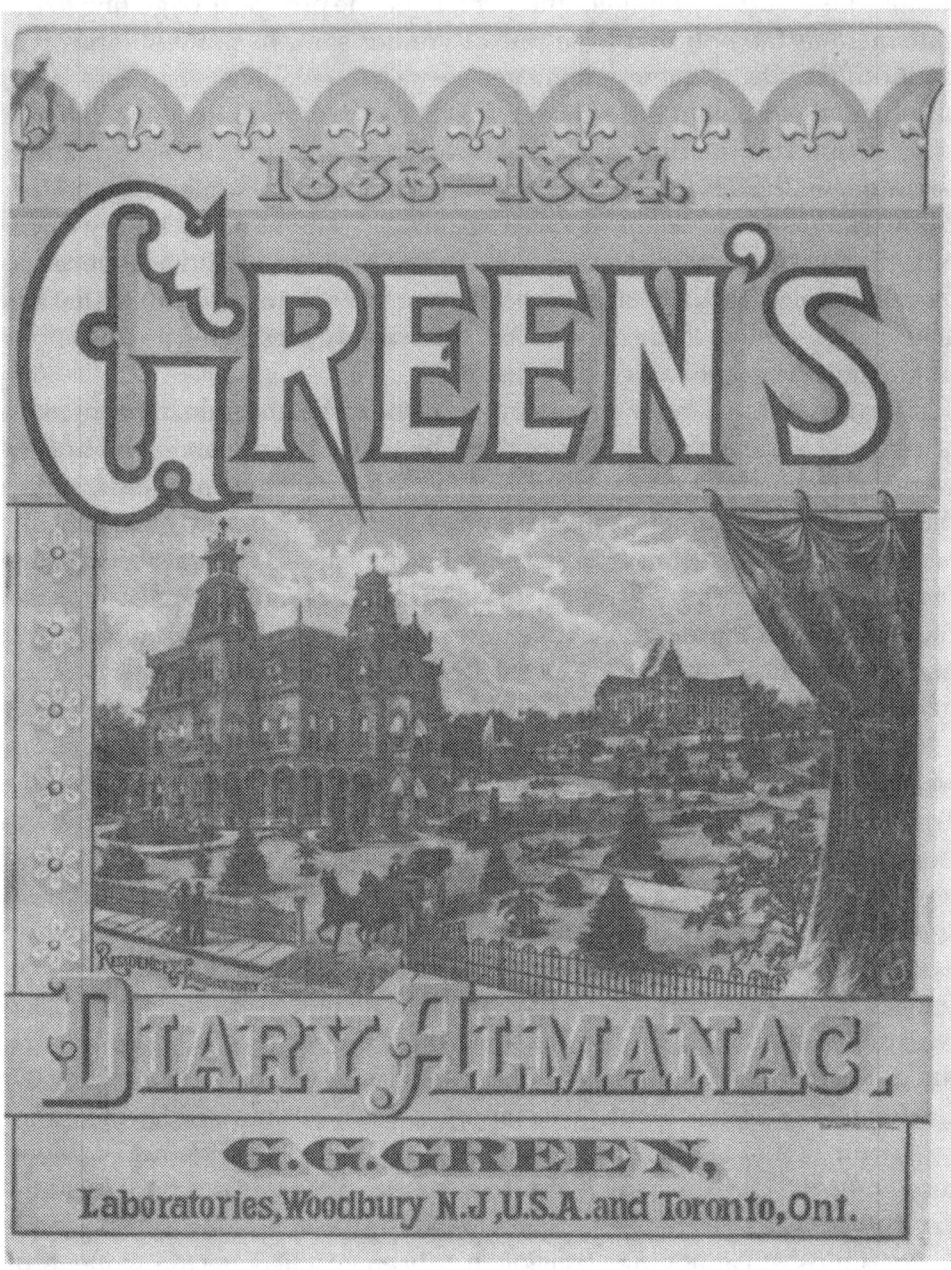

Figure 1. Green's Diary Almanac for 1883–1884. *Almanacs were required reading in the nineteenth century, providing information on the weather, crops, recipes, and especially for those distributed liberally by patent medicine firms, on personal health. Large collections of patent medicine almanacs, such as the one containing more than 1,700 examples recently given to the National Library of Medicine, are most easily catalogued as a complete collection, with finding lists available for those seeking ephemera images. (Courtesy of the author)*

most valuable when ready. In this example, a finding list of names of bookplate owners alone would be able to be used much more rapidly while the scholarly community awaits the more complete result. There is a trade-off, to be sure, between these two methods. The single entry cataloging of complete collections loses a great deal of detail which is essential to the searcher. Thus the one-time cataloging of a collection of valentines would demand looking at each object to find an appropriate image; a finding list alone could be only a starting point.

Costs play the major role in dictating how detailed the cataloging of ephemera images will be. The expenditure to completely catalog a book into RLIN now ranges between $40 and $60; costs for cataloging an image cannot be much less. Several years ago the Bucks County Historical Society received a grant to catalog its commercial ephemera, beginning with 1300 chromolithograph trade cards. (Figure 2) The project called for the recording of 45 different fields, and with the planned system it would be possible, for example, to even distinguish among the types and colors of the flowers illustrated on the cards; because of its expense, the project never got beyond the trade cards.[4] This is not surprising when one considers the size of an average trade card and the limitations on what might be depicted. Such costs cannot be justified for a voluminous collection of images, and many ephemera collections are very large. Indeed, there is almost no possibility that even a medium-sized collection of 10,000 items can be cataloged at reasonable cost and in a reasonable amount of time. In addition to costs, there are other major difficulties in cataloging ephemera; most do not have a title, date, or publisher's name, further explaining why there is so little cataloging of ephemera in public collections. Despite these problems, projects such as the bookplate catalog at the College of Physicians continue to advance. (Figure 3) Under any circumstance, if ephemera is cataloged, only limited information should be included. Practical considerations of time, money and personnel mean that in reality one could never provide access to all the subjects of a picture anyway.[5]

Ultimately one must make a decision among the three conditions which govern most of life's choices—speed, cost, and thoroughness; we can usually have only two of the three. I advocate the rapid minimal concept. As Horace said, "Vitae summa brevis spem nos vetat incohare longam" (Life is too short to allow us to enter into far-reaching hopes).[6] Michael Winship affirmed this feeling, commenting that he often worries

> at the amount of detail that sometimes creeps into cataloging records. The correct amount of detail is a matter of judgment and will vary according to a library's resources and collection strengths, but too much detail may conceal the very piece of

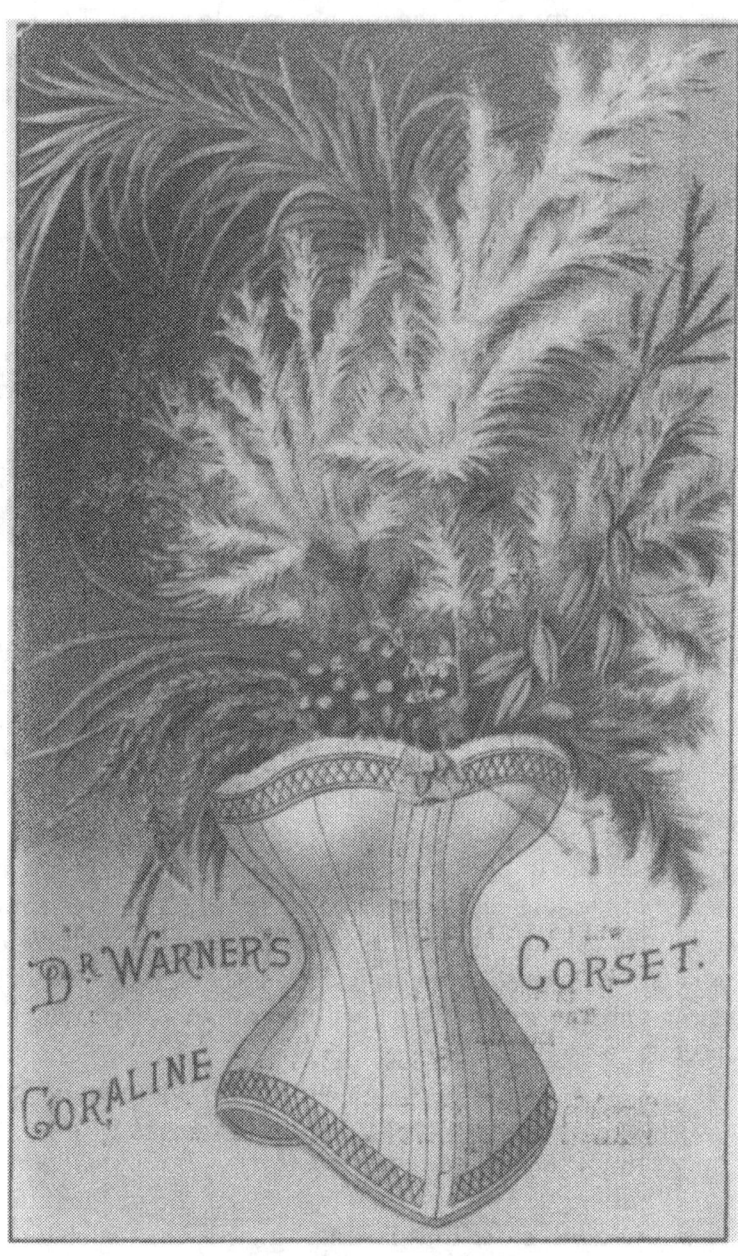

Figure 2. Chromolithograph Trade Card for Dr. Warner's Coraline Corset. *Other than posters, such trade cards were the only available method for marketers to use color in their advertisements in the late nineteenth century, and they are often in demand as novel illustrations. (Courtesy of the author)*

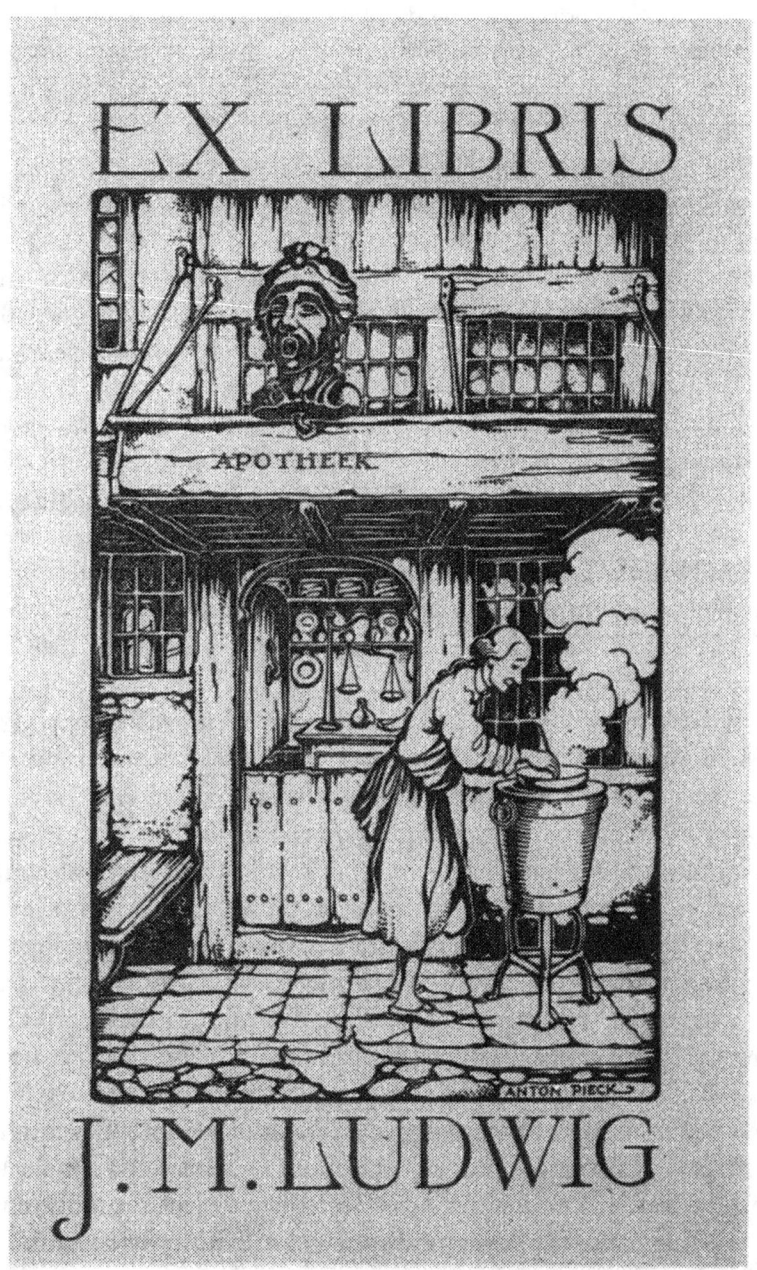

Figure 3. Bookplate of J. M. Ludwig by Anton Pieck. *Large bookplate collections, such as the recently acquired group of more than 12,000 medical bookplates at the College of Physicians of Philadelphia, need cataloguing by owner, artist, and subject at the minimum, for the wealth of detail they can provide is approached in a variety of ways by searchers. (Courtesy of the author)*

information that is most relevant. A cataloging record will never reproduce the text in its entirety or satisfy the scholar's needs for the original, nor can it provide access by every possible point of scholarly interest.[7]

Instead, Winship advocated short, accurate, and clear records of a library's entire holdings over long, elaborated ones that conceal, and to some extent cause a tremendous cataloging backlog of inaccessible, and thus generally useless, materials.

Museums differ from libraries in their cataloging, but museums, and especially art museums, are obviously major sources for images of all types. Art museums organize their objects by medium, and generally catalog each item individually. Because these objects are housed in separate departments; prints, paintings, sculpture, decorative arts, etc., the search for individual images is often difficult. The fundamental obstacle in retrieving information from images in museums derives from the traditional way great collections have been organized by medium rather than by content. In formal art history the methods of organization used are artists, schools, and methods of reproduction; save by the stored-up memory, often extensive, of curators, it is not possible to discover an image by what its title happens to be.[8]

There are no separate departments in museums for ephemera, and such material can often be found in more than one location. Libraries and librarians have learned to cooperate with each other and have institutionalized mutually advantageous programs such as RLIN and OCLC, but museums and curators have not as yet been able to develop a comparable system. Further, few museums have yet been able to develop acceptable systems for the entire museum to which their individual departments would willingly subscribe. However, a number of prototype projects are under way to develop systems for museums similar to RLIN, and as a first step, commercially available collection management systems are now available.[9]

A subject index is the ideal for every one who looks for images, but it is rare to find one that is adequate. Subject indexing is a subjective task. With no acceptable system for consistently determining subject content, many museum curators are reluctant to provide subject indexing for their collections. A major problem is the seemingly impossible task of finding verbal equivalents for pictorial content, verbal language being obviously inadequate for expressing visual language. Words are never more than crude approximations for images.[10] Certainly the identification of objects and actions, times and places, in a picture, depends on the background and experience of the indexer. There is no substitute for an educated eye to see if access should be provided to a particular attribute. A collector or researcher searching for special images may find things in a picture that both the average person, and the trained cataloger, will probably not find. A close friend, the late physician Gerald Rodnan, assembled a superb collection of prints on gout; he could find gout in certain prints that no one else would possibly discover. The Philadelphia Museum of Art listed medical subjects as being in 99 of more than 10,000 searches in a recent cataloging project of French eighteenth and nineteenth century prints; I am sure that I would have found five times as many. A botanist would most certainly uncover more examples of botanical subjects than I would using the same collection. Several collections use a fixed number of subject headings, providing some limitation on the large number of possibilities which might otherwise exist. For example, the National Museum of American Art uses 41 subjects for its images, and the Yale Center for British Art uses a database program with 38 subject areas.[11] Ultimately it may be possible to reduce subjectivity by having a computer, a truly objective analyst, analyze a picture to list its subjects, but for now computers are capable only of properly determining color and certain abstract forms.[12]

The fact remains that the accurate identification of subject matter is a problem endemic in art history, a major reason being that there are various levels of describing subjects. David W. Scott cites the example of Picasso's *Three Musicians*, in the collection of the Museum of Modern Art in New York City, asking "What indeed is the subject matter of the picture? All shapes are highly distorted and abstracted, but there appear to be three seated figures wearing costumes and masks. Two hold musical instruments and the third, a musical score. There also appears to be table in the foreground with objects on it and a dog in the background. These figures, the author notes, could just as well be "actors," or "masks" or a "pierrot, harlequin and monk." He also raises a question of whether the score held by one of the musicians might more properly be an accordion; it is difficult to say.[13] The distinguished art historian Erwin Panofsky, cited four levels of subjects in art, ranging from what the objects in the image are, to what they mean, and what they symbolize. A portrait of a woman with a child could be just that, or a depiction of the Madonna or even a statement of maternal love. At times the portrait may be all of the above, but if so, this information is not too easily noted in a subject file. Further, the same image often represents different kinds of subject, and viewers conceive of illustrations in varied ways. For example, the engraving of Rembrandt's well-known portrait of Dr. Ephraim Bonus is at the same time a good idea of what Dr. Bonus looked like, a good idea of what Rembrandt's creative abilities could produce, and a reproduction of an important Rembrandt print.[14] Thus one image can represent the subject of a work, the work itself, and the work represented in another work. The same levels of ambiguity in determining the subject in a fine-arts image are evident with ephemera images as well.

Searchers for images are generally concerned with content, not with form. Most often the search is for a picture in any form, and the searcher may not care if it is a painting, print, photograph, valentine, or poster, nor is there concern over the source, be it a book, journal, or pamphlet. Even if a particular research topic makes large scale use of single sheets of printed paper or other material that might be described as 'ephemera,' only in special cases will it matter that the material is defined in this way.[15] For these searchers, the best sources would be picture collections, such as those at the New York Public Library or the Free Library of Philadelphia, or any library of images which is organized by subject rather than by form. It is not surprising that for these searchers, the holdings of art museums are frequently difficult to access. Of course, if the artist's name is known, the problem is simplified, for museums organize their collections in this way. But if the subject of the search is a balloon ascension, a group of porpoises, or any other specific subject, the task is considerably more difficult. While searchers often want illustrations that relate closely to their subject, it is often the case that context is not at all important. In fact, the desired image may be one to be used for the background for a display or a piece of artwork for a label; in such cases the searcher would completely ignore the original context of the illustration.[16]

Search techniques are often creatively developed, and generally make use of special collections where there is a good likelihood of finding an appropriate image, instead of a general picture collection. In Washington, D.C., one goes to the National Library of Medicine for a medical image and to the Air And Space Museum for an image of a biplane. There are special libraries which cater to searchers looking for images from ephemera sources; major repositories for such material include the Landauer Collection at the New-York Historical Society, the Burdick Collection at the Metropolitan Museum in New York, the Curt Teich Postcard Archives in Wauconda, Illinois, and the John Johnson Collection in the Bodleian Library in Oxford. There are approximately 100 thematic categories of products and services into which the more than 850,000 items in the Landauer Collection are divided, but new subject areas are added from time to time; recently created groups include several which Mrs. Landauer never would have thought of such as AIDS, the Environment and Recycling.[17] The Johnson Collection is even larger, containing more than 1.5 million items broken into approximately 700 categories, the long list including such detailed subjects as Esperanto, Hieroglyphic Letters, Walking Races, and Tobacco Papers.[18] The Teich Collection of more than 350,000 postcard images is divided into 164 major and 1810 minor subject categories and is computer indexed. There are, for example, 62 categories under "Advertising," including jewelry, auto supplies, resorts and drug stores.[19] Obviously, these are perfect collections in which to search for novel ephemera images.

But they are, of course, not the only ones, and frequently general picture collections will provide excellent material. Here again, a good subject index to a general collection would increase access considerably, as it would to a special collection, for users can often find appropriate material in unlikely places. There are good images in the picture files of the National Library of Medicine that could fill all sorts of needs; as the former curator of this collection wrote,

> "… visual element cataloging can potentially increase access to still picture collections, nearly all of which are specialty collections, but which usually have many images of general interest, applicable to other uses totally unrelated to the collection's publicized narrow scope."[20]

And even if subject indexes do not exist, there are other access points for searchers who can get into records through authors, titles, series, geographical locations, publishers, dates, and other notes. The list of search techniques should also include the devoted attention of a kind and knowledgeable librarian, curator, or archivist, often the most effective means of pointing the way to an appropriate image. But even these alternative catalog access points, while useful in a searching strategy, do not always work; at times access to subjects must be there. For example, the Library of Congress found that their rare pamphlet collection could be made much more valuable with subject access:

> because of characteristics peculiar to 18th- and 19th-century publications, the effectiveness of author or title searching is dramatically reduced. Pamphlets from this time period often have anonymous or pseudonymous authors. Furthermore, the titles of these pamphlets are often lengthy, formulaic, and rarely contain unique retrievable descriptors. No matter what retrieval approaches were tried, the results seldom proved to be satisfactory for the researcher.[21]

Why ephemera? Why would searchers want ephemera images anyway? The main reason is that such images are often primary source materials, and as such, are invaluable to the scholar in identifying issues of the past. Often such primary sources are most valuable when the purposes for which they were compiled are at the farthest remove from the purpose of the historian.[22] Samuel Foster Haven, librarian of the American Antiquarian Society, writing about broadsides in his semiannual report of 1872, noted that the

> ... posters, advertisements, notices, programs and indeed whatever is printed on one side of a sheet of paper, large or small ... are legitimate representatives of the most ephemeral literature, the least likely to escape destruction, and yet ... the most vivid exhibitions of the manners, arts and daily life, of communities and nations ... They imply a vast deal more than they can literally express, and disclose visions of interior conditions of society such as cannot be found in formal narratives.

A great deal of contemporary research depends on material outside of books and serials; it uses manuscripts, films, TV, and ephemera as well. For example, in his definitive study of the American medicine show, the author Brooks MacNamara made extensive use of a scrapbook, which may have been assembled by a showman who styled himself The Great Cummings or Diamond Bill Cummings Ph.D., and which contains about 80 pages of clippings, labels, flyers, and other medicine show items, most of which appear to date from the first quarter of the twentieth century.[23]

Among the items cited from the scrapbook was a receipt for a $2.00 license given to a pitchman in Burlington, Vermont, in 1922, so that he could sell his liniment; a contract form sent by the Oregon Indian Medicine Company in advance to prospective hotels for the lodging of its traveling teams; and handbills offered to purchasers of its products by the German Medicine Company for the purpose of building attendance for sales presentations. There is no reason why this material should have been kept, but thanks to its availability, our knowledge of the medicine show is now much more nearly complete than it might have been.[24]

A second major reason for the use of ephemera images is that they can be provocative, fresh and exciting because they are new. Readers do tire of standard illustrations used over and over again in books and magazines, and the rarity of novel images assures increased readership. Picture reference librarians who have carefully listened to patrons to understand the methods by which they request information better, frequently note that readers ask for "dramatic pictures" or "grabbers," stressing that they want an image that is novel and relatively unknown.

Aids to access of ephemera images, fortunately, do exist to facilitate the life of the researcher, and with the progress in the development of computerized systems, more are on the way. Certain of these aids are published, others can be found in special libraries, and newer technological methods are being designed in the form of CD-ROMS, Videodiscs and networks of databases in sources such as the Internet, Compuserve® and America Online®.

Publications include such representative sources as the *Index to Reproductions of European Paintings,* the *World Painting Index* and the *Iconclass System.*[25] There are only 22 paintings listed under the heading of "Medical Themes" in the *Index to Reproductions*, and a number of other subjects are noted as well. References such as the *World Painting Index* are a bit more difficult to use, for they give titles, not subjects. A search requires a three part process: first one finds a possible title, then goes to an Artist List to find the located title and notes a reference; finally one goes to the Reference list to find the particular article in which the reproduction appears. To find a painting of a pharmacy, for example, the search would turn up *Pharmacie* by Marcel Duchamp, *Pharmacy at La Pommade* by F. Boilauges and three paintings entitled *Drug Store* by Edward Hopper, Larry Rivers and K. Tokita.[26] There is, in addition, *Drugstore Cowboys* by R. Fansella. There are limitations to using this source, for unless the title begins with the subject searched, or unless one patiently ploughs through the entire volume, nothing can be found. Titles, of course, are often misleading, and of no value whatsoever in the case of political caricatures, a rich source of forceful ephemera images. Still another useful reference is Iconclass, developed at the Univ. of Leiden by Henri van de Waal and L. D. Couprie, a classification scheme whose underlying principle is the secondary subject matter depicted in works of art; it uses a hierarchical classification that places images depicting related themes in proximity to other images depicting such themes.[27]

The Frick Art Reference Library in New York, the Witt Library in the Courtauld Institute, London, and the Index of Christian Art in Princeton are examples of special image libraries which have extensive photographic files of art classified by artist and subject.[28] The Frick Library has more than 750,000 photographs of which approximately 450,000 have been so classified.[29] While this total contains no prints or ephemera, it does include paintings, drawings, watercolors, illuminated manuscripts and sculpture. It is a simple matter to find many entries on the Annunciation, the Holy Ghost, Saints and Circumcision, but a more difficult task to locate more mundane subjects such as mortars and pestles. There are, for example, more than 160 entries for Cosmas and Damian, the patron saints of medicine and pharmacy, but only 19 for dentists. Similar search results could be expected from a study of the Witt photographic collection, which contains 1.6 million reproductions of European paintings by 75,000 artists, or from the Index of Christian Art, a superb resource which includes more than 400,000 records of images before 1400, and thus contains nothing printed on paper and certainly no ephemera at all.[30]

But it is the technologically advanced systems using computers, videodiscs, and CD-ROMS which provide the most promising means of accessing images. Many already exist, others are being developed and still more are in the planning stage. A twelve inch videodisc can store 55,000 images; if both sides are used twice as many could be included.[31] The National Library of Medicine videodisc project exemplifies the utility of this new research tool; its videodisc will store 55,000 images of objects in its collection; photographs, prints, posters, advertisements, trade cards, postcards, comic valentines and other print media will be included. (Figure 4) Used with a computerized database system, one will be able to quickly find appropriate images for subjects searched, and requests can be made for two or more subjects to narrow the number of objects located.[32] Because of the variety of images contained, the completed project will be a boon to all those who want exciting dramatic illustrations, as opposed to more common examples. Estimates of costs to prepare the NLM videodisc are about five to seven dollars for each of the images and four dollars for the entry of each into the database, totaling about ten dollars per image. It has taken about six months to make this videodisc and four years to prepare the database. Thus the creation of the videodisc with its 55,000 images costs about $550,000![33] Even though costs would be expected to decline in the future, the labor necessary to develop the system would seem to preclude any extensive recording of ephemera collections on videodiscs. The Wellcome Library in London is also preparing a videodisc of its medical images, the Bibliothèque Nationale working with the Pergamon Press has prepared one of 38,000 images of the French Revolution, the Smithsonian Institution has made a videodisc of 55,000 of its railroad photographs, the Avery Library at Columbia University has made a videodisc (Aviador) of 45,000 architectural drawings in its collection, The National Agricultural Library has one of photographs from the Forest Service, and the Air and Space Museum has one of photographs of planes.[34] This hardly exhausts the list, for there are many more, new ones being published all the time.[35]

A second resource, primarily developed for art museums, art galleries and private collections, provides programs which combine text and image together. The ADMIRa® program, the Vidi-O Image Manager® and Art Stacks® are commercial examples; with these programs one can access information by artist, date, country, collection, subject, etc. and the computer screen shows both the image and related information at the same time.[36]

CD-ROM programs have a distinct advantage over videodiscs in that they are digital systems, capable of being transmitted over long distances. A CD-Rom holds 250,000 pages of text, 7000 photographs or graphics of poor quality, good enough for identification only, or 100 photographs of a quality

The Search for Ephemera Images / 117

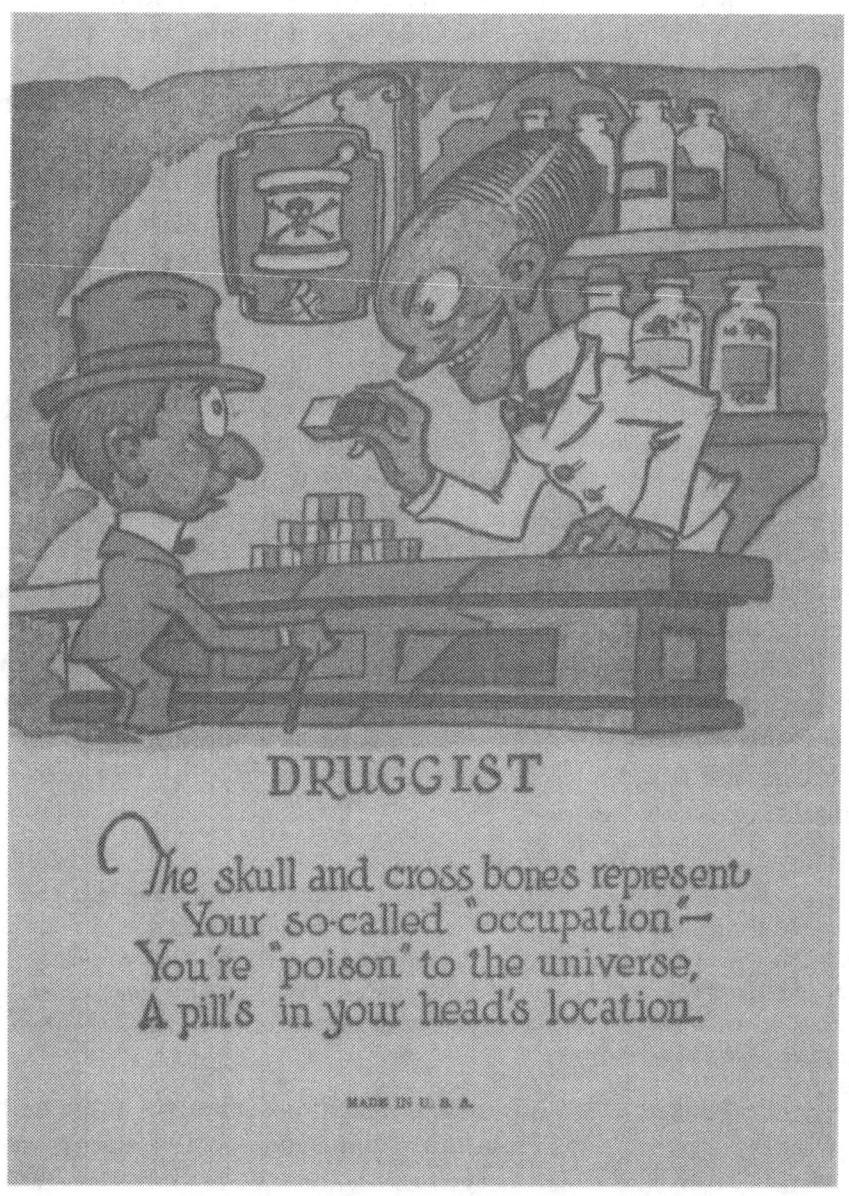

Figure 4. Anonymous Comic Valentine, ca. 1910. Printed ephemera is often an excellent source for uncommon images; this comic greeting in the collection of the National Library of Medicine is one of several meant to be given, anonymously of course, to doctors, dentists, pharmacists, or nurses on Valentines Day. (Courtesy of the author)

good enough for reproduction. Several systems now offer databases of art auction records, but these are not adequately indexed by subject to be useful to the image searcher. Kodak now offers commercially its Photo CD System© for which one needs a special CD player and which can provide 100 high-quality (but still not at the level of 35 mm film) images per disc.[37] The Kodak system is fast; in January, 1993 the Smithsonian prepared a CD-ROM of photographs from the Clinton inauguration within 48 hours, and the resulting disc, "The Inaugural as seen by the Smithsonian Institution," was commercially available within a week. Cornell University is putting books on similar discs, the University of Southern California is putting the Dead Sea Scrolls on one, the Library of Congress has a disc of Matthew Brady photographs on one and is developing a disc of its American political caricatures as well. There are many more.

The future will bring still more exciting and useful tools for the searcher of images of all types, including ephemera images. It is already possible to use computer networks such as the Internet to search through multiple databases, several of which include images, although the number of ephemera images on such networks is, and for some time will continue to be, small. The prospect of developing common formats for searching images remains a daunting one. Other intriguing ideas are under development as aids for access to images, and one can even begin to speculate on imaginative solutions. For example, pattern recognition is an original concept that could save considerable time for searchers, for it bases a new search on a prototype image that is fed into the computer; instructions by words or other commands are not necessary.

> It works something like this. Take a file of images ..., instruct the computer, via a set of programs, to analyze all records that share some common denominator (e.g., analyze all caricatures indexed as Richard Nixon) ... The computer would sort through and analyze each of these records, coming up with a kind of digital, iconographic fingerprint of Richard Nixon. Now, if there are any caricatures of Richard Nixon in the next batch of scanned images, the computer can automatically index them, based on its recognition of a known pattern.[38]

But another concept is even more far reaching. With the availability of computer programs such as Photoshop© which enable designers to manipulate photographs and other designs on the computer, one can create any desired image. Here the searcher, or designer, starts with a found image and adds or subtracts parts of it to create the unique illustration needed. With this concept, now available to everyone, it may not be necessary any longer to search in any library, collection or museum; one just sits at the keyboard and creates. Whether this will turn out to be a boon to all mankind or not, or even a boon to just those looking for simplified access to unique images, remains to be seen.

NOTES

1. Alan Clinton, *Printed Ephemera: Collection, Organization, Access* (London: Clive Bingley, 1981), p. 40.
2. Catalogs published by the Ephemera Society of America, Inc., Box 37, Schoharie, NY 12157 and the Ephemera Society, 12 Fitzroy Square, London W1P 5HQ, England, provide names, addresses and themes and categories collected for each member (individual, dealer or institution) listed.
3. Suzy Taraba, "Administering the Cataloging of Special Collections Materials," *Rare Books and Manuscripts Librarianship*, 7, no. 2 (1992), p. 88.
4. Fields included: collection, catalog number, number of items, accession no., former number, source, date acquired, reference, publisher, condition, size, size of images (2), date of item, date of original, medium (4), reproduction, subject (3), title (2), index term, description, design code (2), border, artist (2), engraver, lithographer, photographer, printer, publisher, publication, vendor, business address, other names, locations (2), background text, additional information. Not all of the fields were used in tabulated reports.
5. Sara Shatford, "Analyzing the Subject of a Picture: a Theoretical Approach," *Cataloging & Classification Quarterly*, 6, no. 3 (1986), p. 54.
6. Clinton, p. 44.
7. Michael Winship, "What the Bibliographer Says to the Cataloger," *Rare Books & Manuscripts Librarianship*, 7, no. 2 (1992), p. 102.
8. Clinton, p. 59.
9. Nancy S. Allen, "The Museum Prototype Project: A View from the Library," *Library Trends*, 37, no. 2 (1988), p. 180.
10. Thomas H. Ohlgren, "The Bodleian Project: Computer Cataloguing and Indexing Medieval Illuminated Manuscripts and Early-printed Books." *First International Conference on Automatic Processing of Art History, Data and Documents, Pisa, 4–7 September, 1978*, Vol I, no. xv, p. 11.
11. Karen Markey, *Subject Access to Visual Resource Collections* (Westport, Conn.: Greenwood Press, 1986), p. 125–6; Anne Marie Logan, *Computerized Indexing of British Art, First International Conference on Automated Processing of Art History Data and Documents, Pisa, 1978*, Vol. II, p. 217–34.
12. Shatford, p. 57.
13. David W. Scott, "Museum Data Bank Research Report: the Yogi and the Registrar," *Library Trends*, 37, no. 2 (1988), p. 132.
14. Sara Shatford, "Describing a Picture: A Thousand Words Are Seldom Cost Effective," *Cataloging and Classification Quarterly*, 4, no. 4 (1984), pp. 18–19.
15. Clinton, p. 17.
16. Lindsay Howe, "The Use of Optical Disc for Archival Image Storage," *Archives and Manuscripts*, 18, no. 1 (1990), p. 103.
17. Wendy Shadwell, "Bella C. Landauer Collection of Business & Advertising Art at the New-York Historical Society," *Cameo Cards & Bella C. Landauer* (Schoharie, NY: Ephemera Society of America, 1992), pp. 62–3.
18. *John Johnson Collection of Printed Ephemera: Main Subject Headings* (Oxford: Bodleian Library, 1990).
19. Christine A. Pyle, "Now Entering American History," *Lake County Museum Postcard Journal*, 4, no. 2 (1987), p. 2.
20. Lucinda H. Keister, *User Types and Queries: Impact on Image Access Systems* (1991), p. 10. (unpublished manuscript)
21. Belinda D. Urquiza, "A Current Library of Congress Project for Cataloging 19th-century Imprints," *Rare Books & Manuscripts Librarianship*, 7, no. 2 (1992), p. 93.
22. Maurice Rickards, *Collecting Printed Ephemera* (London: Phaidon & Christies Ltd., 1988), p. 18.
23. Brooks MacNamara, *Step Right Up* (Garden City, NY: Doubleday, 1972).
24. William H. Helfand, "Pharmaceutical Ephemera," in George A. Bender and John Parascandola,

Historical Hobbies for the Pharmacist (Madison: American Institute of the History of Pharmacy, 1974), pp. 31–33.

25. Isabel S. Munro and Kate M. Munro, *Index to Reproduction of European Paintings* (New York: H. W. Wilson, 1956); Patricia Pate Havlice, *World Painting Index* (Metuchen, N.J.: Scarecrow Press, 1977).

26. *The World Painting Index* provides three published references to the Hopper painting, Boston Museum of Fine Arts, American Paintings in the Museum of Fine Arts, Boston, 1969; Lloyd Goodrich, Edward Hopper, NY, Abrams, nd, which has a color reproduction; and Three Painters of America, Charles Demuth, Charles Sheeler, Edward Hopper, NY, Arno, 1969.

27. Markey, p. 119. The system itself includes only the names of the iconographic themes related to each subject, or, in its Bibliography, books and articles about the theme; those visual resources using the system supply the names of the works of art.

28. There is also an *Index of Jewish Art: Iconographic Index of Hebrew Illuminated Manuscripts*, at the Israel Academy of Science and Humanities in Jerusalem.

29. John Russell, "Trouble at the Nonpareil of Art Libraries," *New York Times*, Arts and Leisure Section (1 March, 1993), p. 35.

30. The Witt collection is in the process of being computerized; the database will use the Iconclass system.

31. Pamela N. Danziger, "Picture Databases: a Practical Approach to Picture Retrieval," *Database* (Aug. 1990), pp. 13–17.

32. For example, a request for 'Advertising' turned up 189 items and a request for 'Drugs' turned up 197. Requesting both together brought 104 matches. Screening through these, it was simple to find appropriate images.

33. Michael Greenhalgh, "Graphical Data in Art History and the Humanities: Their Storage and Display," *History and Computing* 1 (1989), p. 127. This understates present costs: "... the time and money (not to say skill) involved in preparing an analog Videodisk of 108,000 images, with its concomitant database, could easily exceed $150,000."

34. Greenhalgh, p. 127; Steven Vincent, "High Art, High Tech," *Art & Auction*, (Feb. 1993), p. 80; Angela Giral, "At the Confluence of Three Traditions: Architectural Drawings at the Avery Library," *Library Trends*, 37 no. 2 (1988), pp. 232–42.

35. Additional examples are given in Howe, note 16.

36. Greenhalgh, p. 122; Vincent, p. 79.

37. The player costs about $400 and will play audio discs as well as CD-ROM discs. Each disc will hold images taken from three rolls of 36 exposure 35 mm film, and development costs are about $1.00 per image.

38. Gerald Stone, *Archivista: New Technology for an Old Problem, Studies in Multimedia*, nd, p. 158.

Forthcoming...

Art History through the Camera's Lens

Editor
Helene E. Roberts

"Art History Through the Camera's Lens effectively explores the dependent relationship between photography and art history from their beginnings in the nineteenth century, a relationship that also made possible the development of connoisseurship, lectures with paired lantern slides, the critical history of images, and the art book."
—**Richard Brilliant**, Columbia University

"These essays provide a most welcome historical assessment of fundamental aspects of the photography of art."
—**Egbert Haverkamp-Bergemann**, Institute of Fine Arts, New York University

P hotography of art has served as a basis for the reconstruction of works of art and as a vehicle for the dissemination and reinterpretation of art. This book provides the first definitive treatment of the subject, with essays from noted authorities in the fields of art history, architecture, and photography. The essays explore the many meanings of photography as documentation for the art historian, inspiration for the artist, and as a means of critical interpretation of works of art. Art History Through the Camera's Lens will be important reading for students, historians, librarians, and curators of the visual arts.

Documenting the Image Series, Volume III

Fall 1995: Cloth • ISBN: 2-88124-642-7 • $60/£39/ECU50 Paperback • ISBN: 2-88124-643-5 • $24.95/£16/ECU21

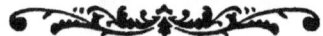

Gordon and Breach Publishers

North/South America: University of Toronto Press, 340 Nagel Drive, Buffalo, NY 14225-4731, USA
Tel: (800) 565-9523 • Fax: (716) 683-4557
Europe: International Publishers Distributor, c/o PO Box 90, Reading, Berkshire RG1 8JL, UK
Tel: +44 (0) 1734 568316 • Fax: +44 (0) 1734 568211
Australia/Asia: International Publishers Distributor, Kent Ridge, PO Box 1180, Singapore 9111
Tel: +65 741 6933 • Fax: +65 741 6922

For Product Safety Concerns and Information please contact our EU representative GPSR@taylorandfrancis.com
Taylor & Francis Verlag GmbH, Kaufingerstraße 24, 80331 München, Germany

www.ingramcontent.com/pod-product-compliance
Lightning Source LLC
Chambersburg PA
CBHW082337220526
45470CB00008B/2546